AF663212

Redefining Relationships in Romans

Biblical Hermeneutics Rediscovered

The Series as the name suggests will focus on Biblical Hermeneutics, i.e., literary works concerned with methods of interpreting the Old and New Testaments of Bible via different stream of topics like Literature & Poetry, Indigenous Philosophizing, Ethical response towards Ecology, Health & Healing, Science & Technology, Feminist Theology, Sociological approach towards Human Rights, Law & Politics, Arts, History of Ideas, Ancient Civilizations, Cultural Contiguity, Religious Cosmologies & Mysticism, Appraisal of various Theologians, World Peace & Harmony, Global Capitalism, Network Marketing, Cybertheology, Population & Demographics, Epigraphic Studies, Contextualized Education, and many others. We welcome a Mss. on any topic/s mentioned, whether they are original works, scholarly monographs, collections of conference papers, revised dissertations, or translations of historical documents. Through the Series we, the Publishers, are striving to put forward published works that may help Institutions, Academic Bodies, Researchers, Scholars and the World at large in furthering their respective knowledge and understanding on the concerned subject. We welcome your comments on our efforts and further suggestions on how we can enshrine new ray of analysing & explaining the written Texts through our upcoming books.

Biblical Hermeneutics Rediscovered - 33

Redefining Relationships in Romans

A Socio-Historical and Political Reading

Zakali Shohe

Christian World Imprints

© Zakali Shohe

First Published in 2020 by

Christian World Imprints
Christian Publishing & Books from India
C-3, Wazirpur Industrial Area
Delhi-110052
cwidelhi2017@gmail.com
www.ChristianWorldImprints.com
Phone: +91 11 41526079

ISBN: 978-93-5148-465-3 (HB)
ISBN: 978-93-5148-466-0 (PB)

All rights are reserved. No part of this publication can be reproduced, distributed, performed, publicly displayed, stored in a retrieval system, made into a derivative work, transmitted or utilized in any form or by any means; electronic, mechanical, photocopying, recording or any information storage system, without the prior written permission of the copyright holder(s), as indicated, and the publishers.

Jurisdiction: Any conflict or dispute in relation to this publication shall be adjudged in accordance with the laws of India and the matter shall be subject to the jurisdiction of the Courts, Tribunals or any other Forums of New Delhi, India, only.

Disclaimer: The views, facts, contents, any copyright material used and analysis arrived at in this publication are solely of the Author(s) who assert/s the right to be identified as Author(s); the Publisher does not take any responsibility for the same in any manner whatsoever.

Printed in India.

Contents

Foreword

In this fine study, Zakali Shohe re-reads Paul's Epistle to the Romans in a relational perspective. She analyses how Christ believers of different origin and status constituted faith communities, and how they are related to each other within the wider context of the values and structures of the Roman Empire. Her approach to Paul is well informed by the so-called New Perspectives on Paul. This sharpens her analysis of Pauline passages for their societal dimensions and for the essential social dimension of the gospel of Christ. Situating the Epistle to the Romans consequently within Roman society brings this ancient letter back to life. Her approach enables her to draw conclusions from her study for tackling burning issues of present times, that is in Northeast India and the global COVID-19 pandemic. As much as Romans were relevant to Paul's particular addressees in the first century and at certain junctures in history, as much it is still inspiring for facing today's challenges, in both local and global perspectives.

In Pauline Epistles he brings fundamental insight into the meaning of gospel as the message of Christ that puts into effect the crossing of societal boundaries that divide people of different status and origin. A common text is Galatians 3:28. The usual translation of the verse, however, is misleading and clouds the intended meaning: "There is neither Jew nor Greek, there is neither slave nor free, there is neither male nor female; for you are all one in Christ Jesus" (RSV). In the context of the discussion in Galatians, this rendering does not make good sense. For in Antioch (Gal 2:11-21), as in the Galatian communities, there were Jews and Greeks, slaves and free persons, men and women. Their distinctness is not transcended. The question at stake in these faith communities was how their members as Jews and Greeks, slaves and free persons, men and women could constitute a faith community that makes transparent *dikaiosynētheou*, that is, the *justice of God* who is not partial, but who, in Christ, has included all of humanity in His covenant with His people. In order to bring out the *meaning* of Galatians 3:28 in the narrow context of verses 25-29, I render itas follows:

(25) Since the faith has come, however, we are no longer under a custodian. (26) For you all are sons (and daughters) of God by means of the faith (that you have) in Christ Jesus. (27) For as much as you have been baptized into Christ, you have put on Christ – (28) *regardless if as* Jew or Gentile, as slave or free person, as male or female. For *you* all are (joined together as) one in Christ Jesus. (29) But since *you* belong to Christ, it follows that you are progeny of Abraham, that is, heirs according to the promise.

Paul denies any exclusivist claim to salvation or justice. This understanding of the function of the motif *dikaiosynētheou* in Paul has been emphasised by Hendrikus Boers and other proponents of the New Perspective on Paul.[1] According to this understanding of gospel, the justice of God and his salvation have been extended universally. This does not require a change of identity on the part of the believers. A Greek gentile does not have to become a Jew in order to be counted as a member of the Christ believing community. All individual members should be regarded as a child of God with divinely bestowed gifts and

---

[1] Cf. Hendrikus Boers, The Justificationofthe Gentiles. Paul's letters to the Galatians and Romans, Peaboy/MA 1994.

abilities for the formation of the faith community.[2] Of course, as people of different ethnic origin, gender and societal status form a faith and living community changes in power, attitude and identity will gradually evolve. If this occurs, the promised justice of God in Christ might become transparent. The epistles of Paul were written to overcome divisions and conflicts within the faith communities of people who would not intermingle as equals in the wider society. Daniel Boyarin correctly attributes the imperialist attitude of much of Christianity in church history up to present times to an interpretation of Galatians 3:28 that denies the right of others to exist as others. I would, however, contest that this is what Paul intended.

Cross-cultural processes represent a central feature of the spread of early Christianity; as such, they were the outcome of a widespread understanding of the meaning of gospel in the first century as essentially implying the crossing of boundaries. The divine promise and the prospect of faith and living communities driven by a quest for justice and equality proved quite attractive in antiquity. This social, economic and ethical dimensions of the gospel inspired religious and secular liberation movements throughout history.

This important study of Zakali Shohe reminds us of the societal relevance of the fundamental insight of Paul into the meaning of gospel, that is, as Christians we are called to search for the realisation of communities where difference is appreciated because the Christian ethos is informed by the gospel values of love, honour, and hospitality.

Prof. Dr. Werner Kahl
Missionsakademie an der Universität Hamburg

---

[2] Cf. Daniel Boyarin, A Radical Jew. Paul and the Politics of Identity, Berkeley and Los Angeles 1994.

Acknowledgements

I want to express my deepest gratitude to those who have helped to bring this work to its completion.

To Professor Dr. Werner Kahl, Missionsakademie an der Universität Hamburg for his careful and critical reading and suggestions. I am also thankful to Prof. Kahl for writing the foreword.

To Professor Dr. Lester Edwin J. Ruiz, Director of Accreditation and Global Engagement, ATS for his stimulating insights and his careful reading and constructive comments. Prof. Ruiz has been and continues to be a source of motivation in my journey as an academician.

To Rev. Dr. Kavito Zhimo, the Principal and the community of Trinity Theological College, Dimapur for the rich learning experiences.

To Christian World Imprints, Delhi for publishing this research.

To my mother, my sister and my brother-in-law, my brothers and sisters-in-law for always being there for me and supporting me, and without whose encouragement I would never have come this far in life and in my career.

At the same time I take full responsibility for any shortcomings of the research.

Zakali Shohe

Abbreviations

AB	The Anchor Bible
BDAG	A Greek-English Lexicon of the New Testament and other Early Christian Literature
EDNT	Exegetical Dictionary of the New Testament
ICC	International Critical Commentary
JBL	Journal of Biblical Literature
JCCC	Johnson County Community College
JSNT	Journal for the Study of the New Testament
JSNTSup	Journal for the Study of the New Testament Supplementary Series
NICNT	The New International Commentary of the New Testament
NTS	New Testament Studies
SBL	The Society of Biblical Literature
SBLDS	The Society of Biblical Literature Dissertation Series

SNTS MonographSer	Society for New Testament Studies Monograph Series
TDNT	Theological Dictionary of the New Testament
WBC	Word Biblical Commentary

Chapter 1

Introduction

The identity of any people, group, or community is rooted in its ethnic traditions and practices. They are an integral component of defining an individual, in defining our relationship with one another and to the larger society. The cultural, traditional practices classify and impose diverse aspects of life and its influence within the closed community or the larger society is profound. Positive relationships are important for the well-being of an individual, community, and the larger society. In a situation of conflict, it becomes necessary to use restorative approaches to address behaviors, and attitudes that undermine community connectedness and wellbeing. The beliefs, practices, behaviors, and attitudes of every individual are important in the creation of a relational culture. It affects an individual's connection with other members of the community and the community's connection with the larger society. Relationships are built and it needs nurturing to be deep-rooted and to grow as we find in both lateral and hierarchical relationships that require trust and acceptance. In the present times, we are witnessing the context of multiplicities that exist in our ethnic communities, faith communities, wider societies, and our world. This entails the redefining of relationships, which must not be construed as a call for the renunciation of their old identities and roles. Rather, it is about being considerate of the well-being of an individual, the community, society, and nature. It demands to redefine the believer's relationship with God and fellow human beings. As in society so in the Bible and biblical times there is an emphasis on social, political, cultural, and religious identities and role. To this end, the study explores Romans 12:1-13:10 and Roman 15:7-13 to bring out Paul's exhortation on the roles of the Christ believing community. Following this aim, I will avoid a detailed discussion of every exegetical issue arising from the pericope. Instead, I will concentrate on the identities and roles in redefining relationships.

Identities and Roles

The shift from an individualist to a community-oriented interpretation of Pauline theology is an important contribution since the onset of the sociological approach.[1] On the question of community identity or interpreting Paul as a cultural critic, Daniel Boyarin rejects Paul's Universalism as näive, but at the same time he also recognizes the dangers of insisting on Jewish "difference."[2] There is no doubt that Boyarin presents an intense and engaging reading of Paul. Nevertheless, the danger in Boyarin's interpretation is his conviction that Paul's desire for an ideal universal society beyond difference and hierarchy is motivated by a Hellenistic desire for one, i.e., universal human essence.[3] This, combined with "Hebrew monotheism" made Paul interpret Christ as ushering sameness.[4] The view that Paul's system required the eradication of all human cultural specificities is not convincing. Perhaps Boyarin arrives at this conclusion because he

---

[1] This stands in contrast to a Bultmannian existential reading of Paul.

[2] Daniel Boyarin, *A Radical Jew: Paul and the Politics of Identity* (Berkeley: University of California Press, 1994), p. 6.

[3] Boyarin, *A Radical Jew*, pp. 7-8.

[4] Boyarin, *A Radical Jew*, pp. 9, 156.

looks at Paul through the lenses of Galatians 3:28.[5] Taking into account Romans 12:1-15:13, especially in considering identity and community, such an interpretation of Paul can sideline themes like accepting and accommodating one another.[6]

In contrast, John Barclay offers an alternative perspective for reading Paul in a multicultural age. According to Barclay, Paul relativizes circumcision by calling for "faith working through love" (Gal. 5:6), and he rightly states that faith and love are given shape in the life of a community (Gal. 5:13-6:10). Likewise, in the Roman churches the distinction in food and drink does not define the communities, but Paul replaces them with "righteousness, peace and joy in the Holy Spirit" (Rom. 14:17). These principles are to have an immediate impact on their common life as well as common meals (Rom. 14:1-15:6). Barclay believes that Paul's allegorization of the Jewish particulars is not an attempt to create a "universal human essence" (contra Boyarin), instead, it is to "enable an alternative form of community," which could bridge divisions by "creating new patterns of common life."[7] In this sense, Paul relativizes "cultural specificities," yet, Paul does not present the gospel as if it carries a whole new cultural package, designed to eradicate and replace all others. It is rather a cluster of values, focused on love, which enables the creation of a new community in which varied cultural traditions can be practiced.

---

[5] As also observed by Werner Kahl, such universalist position becomes problematic in the context that spiritualizes differences. For the history of interpretation especially the mission history misunderstood Paul as denying cultural differences, i.e., the eradication of "the other." These interpretations justify Boyarin's concern, but not Paul [Werner Kahl, "Transgressing Boundaries: The Need for Intercultural Biblical Hermeneutics," *New Perspectives on Intercultural Reading of the Bible*, eds. Daniel S. Schipani, Martien Brinkman & Hans Snoek (Elkhart, Indiana: A-VU University Amsterdam & Institute of Mennonite Studies, 2015), p. 183 n. 8].

[6] Zakali Shohe, *Acceptance Motif in Paul: Revisiting Romans 15:7-13* (Frankfurt: Peter Lang, 2017).

[7] John M. G. Barclay, "'Neither Jew nor Greek:' Multiculturalism and the New Perspective on Paul," *Ethnicity and Bible*, ed. Mark G. Brett, Biblical Interpretation Series. Vol. 19 (Leiden/New York/ Köln: E. J. Brill, 1996), p. 210.

In the Pauline epistles, especially in Galatians, Romans, and First and Second Corinthians, many Pauline discourses revolve around the issue of Jewish practices. This is connected directly or indirectly to identity, whether non-Jews who are included in the covenant promises should adopt Jewish practices. In this regard, the Epistle to the Romans proffers the idea of an inclusive community. This entails the redefining of relationships, which must not be construed as a call for the renunciation of their old identities and roles. Instead, it is about redefining the believer's relationship with God and fellow human beings.

To be sure, Paul does not directly use words like "multiple identities" and "roles" in referring to the believers in Christ. Still, the idea that as followers of Christ, believers continue to belong to the world and participate in the public and private spheres is conspicuous in the Epistle to the Romans. The notion of identifying the roles of the believers in Christ is found in Romans 12:1-13:10.[8] From Paul's exhortation in Romans 12:1-13:10 we can highlight the three spheres of the believer's life: the individual sphere (12:1-2), the Christ believing community (12:3-13), and the social and civil/political sphere (12:14-21; 13:1-10). The first sphere, i.e., the individual sphere in this study refers to a personal level, a personal faith, and belief in relating to God. The second sphere is the community of the believers in Christ, especially in relating to one another and growing together as a faith community.

---

[8] Apart from Romans 12:1-13:10 the notion of multiple identities is also present in Romans 8. Paul in Romans 8 does not explicitly use the terms multiple identities in the context of the Spirit. But he states that it is the Spirit that guides the believers to a status of "son" (8:14) and "children" (8:16) of God, and as children of God they have the freedom to call God, "abba" father (8:15). The believers are also "heirs of God" and "joint-heirs" with Christ (8:17). Thus, we find that a believer through the guidance of the Spirit receives multiple identities. In interpreting Romans 8:14-17 from the context of the recipients of the epistle as comprising of both the Jews and the Gentiles, we can say that the Jews and the Gentiles are called "sons," "children," "heirs" or joint-heirs" but not at the expense of their identity as Jews and Gentiles. In addition to maintaining their original identity and their identities and roles in the public and private sphere, the Spirit guides them in their relationship with God as children of God, an identity that is specifically reserved for believers in Christ.

The third sphere, i.e., the social sphere concerns the wider society. Here, Paul's exhortation is directed to the believers in Christ in relating to individuals and groups outside the Christian faith communities. While the civil/political sphere concerns the attitudes and obligations of the believers in Christ towards the superior authorities and the Roman rules and regulations. Then, in Romans 15:7-13 Paul underlines the acceptance motif. A believer in Christ continues to belong to the world for he/she is neither removed out of the world nor set back into it.

As such, within the historical context of Romans, this book explores the instructions of Paul in Romans 12-13 and Romans 15:7-13. To this end, the book briefly analyzes the historical context and also the social status in the Greco-Roman society. It then interprets Romans 12-13 and Romans 15:7-13 within the context of multiple identities and roles, which then calls for a redefinition of relationships and also re-interpretation of Romans. After this, it seeks to articulate a hermeneutic that allows for an understanding that takes into account the diverse social status, cultures, ethnic people groups, nature, and so on.

Methodology

This study employs several approaches and draws insights from them: historical, sociological, and political. Since there are limits to these methods when used individually, I am drawing insights from different methodologies with the hope of drawing out a richer understanding of the texts in the context of multiple identities and roles.

I consider that the insights from history and social science can provide a richly textured understanding of Paul and his thoughts. Margaret Y. MacDonald, comments, "Historical and social-scientific modes of interpretation can serve as a means of correction and control for one another." She views that blending historical and sociological analysis would present a "more complete picture of early Christianity."[9] I agree with MacDonald

[9] Margaret Y. MacDonald, *The Pauline Churches. A Socio-historical Study of Institutionalization in the Pauline and Deutero-Pauline writings,* SNTS

that insights from historical and sociological can contribute to correcting and contributing to one another, but it is doubtful if we can trace back and get a complete picture of early Christianity. Probably, we can acquire a more expansive and rich portrayal of early Christianity.

The books of the Bible are ancient texts dealing with history and therefore the interpretation of the text needs a historical approach. By historical approach I mean the text as interpreted in the light of their specific historical context and attempting to draw out the intended meaning of the text. Nevertheless, the New Testament books apart from being historical writings also comprise social detail with texts referring to social relations, social groups, and patterns of behavior. They describe social contexts, concerning diverse persons, and groups, and are shaped by economic, political, and societal circumstances, structure, and procedure. Accordingly, to grasp its meaning and investigate the social dimension of the texts and their contexts, the historical-critical approach needs to be blended with a social analytic approach.[10] John Elliott remarks that social-scientific criticism compliments historical criticism in its analysis of the Biblical text by facilitating historical criticism to engage in its intended task, i.e., to unearth the intention of the Biblical authors within the contours of their environment. Elliott notes,

> Social-scientific criticism of the Bible is that phase of the exegetical task, which analyzes the social and cultural dimensions of the text and its environmental context through the utilization of the perspectives, theory, models, and research of the social sciences. As a component of the historical-critical method of exegesis, social-scientific criticism investigates biblical texts as meaningful configurations of language intended to communicate between composers and the audiences… Social-scientific criticism thus expands the historical-critical method by adding to its

MonographSer. 60 (Cambridge: Cambridge University Press, 1988), pp. 23-24.

[10] John H. Elliott, *What is Social-Scientific Criticism?* (Minneapolis: Fortress Press, 1993), pp. 10-11.

> repertoire of the foci and the operations the perspectives, theory, models, and research of the social sciences in order to enable the reader of the Bible to understand and interpret more adequately the biblical text and their contexts. It is not a method for creating and manufacturing new data but for viewing and understanding all the data available within a new and more comprehensive theoretical framework. It thus serves a "heuristic" function.[11]

For this study, insights will be drawn from social sciences along with the historical method. By employing insights from historical and social methods in the interpretation of Romans I hope to address the issues of multiple identities and roles in Romans 12-13 and 15:7-13. W. R. Domeris suggests that the object of a socio-historical approach to the books in the Bible is to read it from the perspective of the community to which it was written. But today we find limited evidence for reading into any community of the Bible. Thus, there is a need to read between the lines in order to figure out the structure of the community, its symbolic universe, and its history.[12]

Nevertheless, employing sociological and historical approaches does not mean we can grasp the actual historical setting, because there is a lack of evidence. Yet, the deployment of these approaches helps to develop a more expansive understanding of the ancient text and allow us to make the possible conclusion of the description and the message of the text. This for me is enough justification of why I am using insights from different methodologies. Such an approach provides a more textured understating because the texture is important not for accuracy, but for a fuller understanding of the ancient texts.

The study accepts that Romans 12-13 and15:7-13 is directed to a situation where there are differences among the believers in Christ and that believers in Christ are a small faith community

---

[11] Elliott, What is *Social-Scientific Criticism*, pp. 7, and 14.

[12] W. D. Domeris, "Sociology and Social Historical Investigations," *Text and Interpretation. New approaches in the criticism of the New Testament*, eds. P. J. Hartin & J. H. Petzer (Leiden: E. J. Brill, 1991), p. 226.

within the larger Roman imperial context. A Socio-historical approach attempts to discover and explain the intent of a text as a response to a given situation, and the way it stimulates social response on the part of the recipients. Therefore, John H. Elliott's approach of the text analysis with the concepts of "situation" and "strategy" as foci in interpretation will be utilized. He employs these concepts in place of the conventional exegetical concern with "occasion" and "purpose" which are normally envisaged in ideational and theological terms. On the contrary, the "situation" point toward social conditions and interactions that stimulated the writing of the text. Furthermore, "strategy" better communicates the idea that the text was not simply designed to communicate, but to move the audience to a specific social response.[13] I believe the socio-historical approach will help us to better understand the mentioned text as directed to a specific situation.

This study also employs a political reading of Romans. As Neill Elliott in reading Romans differently asserts that, "the themes that dominate Romans are *political* topics." Elliott justifies this stand by showing how throughout the Epistle to the Romans the diverse themes reveal Paul and the believers' communities in Rome were caught up in the currents of the Roman imperial context.[14] In this study the Roman imperial ideologies, especially presented in Romans 12-13 is explored. The political reading of Romans is a recent phenomenon, but it has continued to thrive amid a deep-rooted perspective about the emphasis of Romans. This already common perspective, Neil Elliott rightly put is "the greatest challenge to a political reading of Romans."[15] The dominant perspectives on Romans have been old and new perspectives. The old perspective, i.e., the reformers reading of Romans is set within the context of Judaism with emphasis on

---

[13] Elliott, *What is Social-Scientific Criticism?*, pp. 54-55. Also refer to John H. Elliott, *A Home for the Homeless. A Sociological Exegesis of 1Peter Its Situation and Strategy* (London: SCM Press, 1981).

[14] Neil Elliott, *The Arrogance of the Nations: Reading Romans in the Shadow of Empire* (Minneapolis, MN: Fortress Press, 2008), pp. 6-7.

[15] Elliott, *The Arrogance of the Nations*, p. 8.

work-righteousness. The new perspective on Romans is within the context of the universal gospel of Paul that includes both Jews and the non-Jews and the opposition from the Jews towards Paul's universal gospel. Both perspectives have focused on Judaism, and sidelined the Roman imperial ideologies. However, in the Epistle to the Romans the imperial ideologies are also extensively reflected, and for this we need to read behind the text and read in-between the lines to identify the language and ideology of power. The study, therefore, emphasizes the imperial ideology in Romans 12-13 by doing a political reading of Paul. The conflicts between the Jews and the non-Jews in Romans 15:7-13 is directed to a community of believers. Nonetheless, it also has connections to the broader context of the Roman imperial system and ideology.

The different approaches to this study are considered with the aim of expressing fully Paul's exhortation towards restorative and positive relationships within members of the community of believers in Christ and also within the larger society.

Romans: A Situational Letter

I still uphold the hypothesis along with the majority view, which I did, in my previous work that Romans is written to address a specific situation.[16] The letter reflects divisions and tensions within the communities of the believers in Christ, i.e., Jews and non-Jews. In this study, I will move further by incorporating imperial ideologies in Paul's address within the context of multiple identities and roles, which then calls for a redefinition of relationships. To achieve the intended goal the study is built on the notion that Romans is directed to a specific situation and historical context.

Much contribution has been made on the Romans especially on its purpose,[17] yet the debate continues with no final consensus.

---

[16] Shohe, *Acceptance Motif in Paul: Revisiting Romans 15:7-13*.

[17] C. E. B. Cranfield, *Romans*, ICC, vol. II (Edinburgh: T&T Clark, 1979), 814-823; A. J. M. Wedderburn, *The Reasons for Romans* (Edinburgh: T&T Clark, 1991), Jacob Jervell, "The Letter to Jerusalem," *The Romans Debate*. Revised and expanded edition. Edited by Karl Paul Donfried (1977. Reprint, Peabody:

Scholars agree that Paul's letters are situational, but a few consider the Epistle to the Romans an exception. A few interpreters view it as reflecting past experience.[18] While others interpret Romans as highlighting Paul's journey to Jerusalem,[19] or some regard Romans as an epistle written to clarify his teaching in Galatians.[20] Scholars and interpreters who reject the hypothesis that Romans is a situational letter do so based on the textual problem of Romans 16, the universal character of the content of the Epistle, or some even point to the similarity of the issues found in Galatians and 1Corinthians, or that Paul had never visited Rome and so was unaware of the situation at Romans.[21] However, the standpoint of these scholars does not carry much weight as the content of the epistle point to a different explanation. Apart from it, if Romans is seen only in line with the other epistles, then the distinctive character of the Epistle to the Romans is sidelined. Hence, Romans needs to be interpreted within a particular context. As such, this

---

Hendrickson, 1991); L. Ann Jervis, *The Purpose of Romans: A Comparative Letter Structure Investigation* (Sheffield: JSOT Press, 1991); Joseph Fitzmyer, *Romans: A New Translation with Introduction and Commentary* (The Anchor Bible; New York: Doubleday, 1992); Stanley Stowers, *A Rereading of Romans: Justice, Jews and Gentiles* (New Haven: Yale University Press, 1994); Lo Lung-Kwong, *Paul's Purpose in Writing Romans: The Upbuilding of a Jewish and Gentile Christian Community in Rome* (Hongkong: Alliance Biblical Seminary, 1998).

[18] Cf. Gunther Bornkamm, "The Letter to the Romans as Paul's last will and Testament," *The Romans Debate*, Edited by Karl Paul Donfried (Peabody, Massachusetts: Hendrickson Publishers, 1977). pp. 22-24. J. W. Drane, "Why Did Paul write Romans?" in *Pauline Studies. Essays Presented to Prof. F. F. Bruce on his 70th Birthday*, ed. D. A. Hagner (Exeter: Paternoster Press, 1980), p. 223. A. Nygren, *Commentary on Romans*, trans. C. C. Rasmusser (1944; London: SCM, 1952), p. 8.

[19] Jacob Jervell, "The Letter to Jerusalem." Jouette M. Bassler, *Divine Impartiality: Paul and a Theological Axiom*, SBLDS 59 (Chico: Scholars Press, 1982), pp. 166-168.

[20] Thomas H. Tobin, *Paul's Rhetoric in its Contexts. The Argument of Romans* (Peabody, Massachusetts: Hendrickson Publishers, 2004).

[21] Ref. Drane, "Why Did Paul Write Romans?," p. 211; V. P. Furnish, *The Love Command in the New Testament* (London: SCM, 1972), p. 115.

study attempts to interpret Romans 12-13 and Romans 15:7-13 within the context of a Jew-gentile relationship and the wider imperial context and explore Paul's exhortation on redefining relationships in such a context. Most interpreters treat Romans 12:1-15:13 as a new section in the letter. James Dunn describes Paul's exhortation in Romans 12:1-15:13 as the "outworking of the gospel for the redefined people of God in everyday terms."[22] Joseph Fitzmyer entitles Romans 12:1-15:13 as, "Hortatory section: The demands for upright life in Christ."[23] While Douglas Moo calls it, "The transforming power of the gospel: Christian conduct."[24]

The question regarding the situation of the Epistle to the Romans has been a debate in Pauline scholarship since the approach of Ferdinand Christian Baur that Romans was a response of Paul to the problems within the Roman Christian community.[25] The issue in the Romans Debate is whether the Epistle is addressing the situation of Roman Christians or it is a universal letter, summing up Paul's thought in general.

Firstly, this study will view Romans as addressing a particular situation within the Roman Christian community, i.e., the issue of the Jew-Gentile relationship. The study takes the stand with Suetonius that Claudius expelled the Jews from Rome

---

[22] James D. G. Dunn, *Romans 1-8* (WBC 38_A. Dallas: Word Books, 1988), p. x.

[23] Fitzmyer, *Romans*, p. 637.

[24] Douglas Moo, *The Epistle to the Romans* (NICNT. Grand Rapids: William B. Eerdmans, 1996), p. 35.

[25] Ferdinand Christian Baur, *The Apostle of Jesus Christ. His life and work, his epistles and his doctrine,* vol. I, Trans. Eduard Zeller (1876, Eugene, Oregon: Wipf and Stock Publishers, 2003), pp. 308-365. For this view of Baur also refer to Francis Watson, *Paul, Judaism, and the Gentiles. Beyond the new perspective* (Revised and expanded edition, Grand Rapids, MI: William B. Eerdmans, 2007), p. 163. Wolfgang Wiefel, "The Jewish Community in Ancient Rome and the Origins of Roman Christianity," *The Romans Debate*, Edited by Karl Paul Donfried (Peabody, Massachusetts: Hendrickson Publishers, 1977). Supporting the view of Baur is T. Zahn.

in 49 CE.[26] This expulsion affected the Jewish believers in Christ and probably a few law observant non-Jew believers in Christ who were also exiled because Christian faith is considered to have originated within the Roman Jewish community. Overall, we see that Claudius Edict changed the setting of Christian worship and Christian faith at Rome.

Secondly, along with the edict this study is also built within the context where the Christian faith is a small group within the larger Roman social and political setting. Therefore, believers in Christ needed to be careful and mindful of the Roman practices and its system in maintaining law and order within the empire. This study attempts to show that in such context Paul emphasizes multiple identities and roles of the believers in Christ in relating to one another and with members and groups in the wider society. As such, it is important to situate Romans within its historical context, to which we turn to in the next chapter of this study.

---

[26] Suetonius, *Claudius 25:4*. This incident is also mentioned in Acts 18:2 and Orosius, *Adversus Paganos vii, 6:15-16.*

Chapter 2

Situating Romans within its Historical Context

Relationships in Roman and Greek society depended on the honor-shame nexus. Giving and receiving the honor was an important aspect of the Roman world. The honor was sought after and desired by all individuals belonging to any social status. An individual's place in the society/community/group was also determined by the honor-shame they received within the standards of the society. The honor system was also connected to the practice of gift-giving, which was both public and private.[27] The privileges and status in the Roman social structure were given importance and implemented accordingly. Thus, Christian faith as a minority group within the larger Roman social order and system, Paul calls the believers in Christ to be attentive to the context so that no unwanted situation would result in division within the community members that would attract the attention of the civil authorities, especially after the impact of the Claudian edict upon the believers

[27] The social construes are further elaborated in the following sections.

in Christ. This imperial context is directly and indirectly reflected in Paul's exhortation in the Epistle to the Romans. As such, this chapter will firstly bring out the Claudian edict of expulsion as it contributes to our understanding of the divisions and differences in the Roman Christian faith communities after the return of the expelled Jews and believers in Christ. Secondly, it will examine the social status in Roman society, especially concerning the privileges.

Suetonius Report on Claudius' Roman Edict

The historical report by Suetonius provides information regarding the hypothesis that the Roman believers did not only originate from the larger Roman Jewish community, but also maintained a significant continuity of practice with the Jews in the synagogue.

Suetonius in *Claudius* (*Vita Divi Claudii*) 25.4 offers important, but brief information concerning an anti-Jewish attitude of Claudius. The text reads *Iudaeos impulsore Chresto assidue tumultuantis Roma expulit* (Since the Jews constantly made disturbances at the instigation of Chrestus, he expelled them from Rome.)[28] Other texts that inform us of the Claudian Roman Edict are the Acts of the Apostles (18:2) that mentions Paul's meeting with a couple, named Aquila, who is of the Pontus race and his wife Priscilla. They had come to Corinth because Emperor Claudius had commanded all the Jews to leave Rome. Apart from Acts, two ancient sources provide us with information on the attitude of Emperor Claudius toward the Roman Jews. They are Dio Cassius, *Roman History* (*Historiae Romanae*); and Paulus Orosius, *History against the Pagans* (*Historiae Adversum Paganos*). Dio Cassius in *Roman History* 60.6.6 reports concerning the early years of Claudius' reign that in AD 41 Claudius deprived the Jews of their right to assembly although he makes no mention of any expulsion.[29] In his *History against the Pagans* 7.6.15,

---

[28] Text according to *Suetonius*. vol. II, Translated by J. C. Rolfe. 2 vols. Loeb Classical Library (Cambridge: Harvard University Press, 1997-98).

[29] Text according to Dio Cassius. *Roman History*, Books 56-60, Translated by Ernest Cary. 9 vols. Loeb Classical Library (Cambridge: Harvard University

Paulus Orosius reports that in the ninth year of his reign, Claudius expelled the Jews from Rome.[30]

The fragment that Seutonius cites [*Claudius* (*Vita Divi Claudii*) 25.4] from an undisclosed source provides important information for our understanding of the reception of Christian faith in first-century Rome. As Rainer Riesner notes, "This brief remark is part of a whole series of religious, civil and military-legal measures undertaken by Claudius."[31] The passage of *Claudius* 25.4 could not have been an invention of Suetonius. It is also probable that Suetonius derives this information from another source, such as the imperial archives to which he might have had access.[32] In his report on the expulsion of the Jews by Claudius, Suetonius does not indicate the date, but only provides a reason, i.e., the Jews were constantly creating disturbances at the instigation of *Chrestus*. In reading *Claudius* 25.4 within the context of *Claudius* 25.3-5, we do not find any chronological order, but a topical one, giving no hint of any relative date. The absence of any concrete date on the report by Suetonius leaves the dating by Orosius of AD 49 as the best candidate, but this is contradicted by Dio Cassius who mentions that Claudius did not drive the Jews out, but ordered them, while continuing their traditional mode of life, not to hold meetings. Dio Cassius offers a tradition, which is placed during the first year of Claudius' reign. The possibility is that Dio Cassius and Suetonius are referring to two different events. Claudius banned Jewish meetings at the beginning of his reign, and later when there were constant disturbances he expelled the Roman Jews who created the disturbances.[33]

Press, 1914-1927).

[30] Paulos Orosius, *History Against the Pagans*. http://www.attalus.org/latin/orosius7A.html (accessed on May11, 2014).

[31] Rainer Riesner, *Paul's Early Period. Chronology, Mission Strategy, Theology*, trans. Doug Stott (Grand Rapids: William B. Eerdmans, 1998), p. 162.

[32] Riesner, *Paul's Early Period*, p. 162.

[33] A detailed analysis of all the Texts of Claudius' Roman Edict is found in my work, *Acceptance Motif in Paul*, 55-77. This view is supported by John M. G. Barclay, *Jews in the Mediterranean Diaspora: From Alexander to Trajan*

The historical occasion of *Claudius* 25.4 can be seen in the expression, *impulsore Chresto*.[34] The meaning of the phrase *impulsore Chresto* has been a matter of considerable controversy. Two strands of interpretation dominate. First, the widely accepted position is the "Christianizing interpretation,"[35] i.e., the unrest among the members in the synagogues in Rome. Second, the other position is that it is a Roman policy against the Jews.[36]

Those who take the "Christianizing interpretation," provide different reasons regarding the unrest among the members in the synagogues. According to them the unrest was because of the Jewish rejection of preaching propagating the messiahship of Jesus of Nazareth,[37] or because of the practice of the table fellowship between Jewish and Gentile believers in Christ, which was a

---

(323 BCE-117 CE) (Edinburgh: T&T Clark, 1996), p. 305; E. Mary Smallwood, *The Jews Under the Roman Rule*: *From Pompey to Diocletian. A Study in the Political Relations* (Boston/Leiden: BRILL, 2001), pp. 210-216; Robert Jewett, *Dating Paul's life* (London: SCM Press, 1979), pp. 36-38; Wiefel, "The Jewish Community in Ancient Rome and the Origins of Roman Christianity," p. 94; Josephus, *Jewish Antiquities* 19. 278-291 and *Jewish War* 5. 214-217. Francis Watson proposes that the two events are connected and the prohibition on the synagogue meetings only indicates an initial response to an ongoing problem that resulted in an expulsion in AD 49 (Watson, *Paul, Judaism, and the Gentiles,* pp. 170-172).

[34] Suetonius, *Claudius* 25.4.

[35] Wiefel, "The Jewish Community in Ancient Rome," p. 93; James C. Walters, "Romans, Jews and Christians: The Impact of Romans on Jewish/Christian Relations in First-Century Rome." *Judaism and Christianity in First-Century Rome*, Edited by K. P. Donfried & P. Richardson (Grand Rapids, Michigan: William B. Eerdmans, 1998), p. 177; Smallwood, *The Jews under the Roman Rule*, p. 211; Peter Lampe, *From Paul to Valentinus: Christians at Rome in the First Two Centuries*, Translated by Michael Steinhauser, Edited by Marshall D. Johnson (1989. Reprint, Minneapolis: Fortress Press, 2003), pp. 11-12.

[36] H. Dixon Slingerland, *Claudian Policymaking and the Early Imperial Repression of Judaism at Rome* (USF Studies in the History of Judaism 160. Atlanta: Scholars Press, 1997), pp. 151-168; Elliott, *The Arrogance of Nations*, p. 98.

[37] For this view, refer to, Wiefel, "The Jewish Community in Ancient Rome," p. 93; Smallwood, *The Jews under the Roman Rule*, p. 211; Lampe,

threat to the boundaries of Judaism.[38] Dixon Slingerland takes the position of the Roman policy against the Jews. Having made an intensive study into the Claudian Edict by comparing the syntax of the phrase *impulsore Chresto*, with similar adverbial phrases from Suetonius' *Lives of the Caesars*, Slingerland concludes that the phrase is primarily written to explain why Claudius expelled the Jews and not why Jews caused the disturbance. His reconstruction of Suetonius' report is that the edict is the policy of the emperor against the Jews.[39] This view is unconvincing because it has no documentary support whatsoever. The edict also explains why the disturbances arose among the Jews in the Roman synagogues, i.e., because of *Chrestus*. However, Slingerland is right that the edict explains why Claudius expelled the Jews. Leonard Victor Rutgers argues similarly that the main motive for the Roman authorities to intervene was to suppress unrest.[40] In line with Slingerland and Rutgers, Neil Elliott proposes that a preferable explanation for the cause of the expulsion lies not in a specific action against Jews, but implementation of Roman policy.[41]

Hence, it is likely that Claudius intervened in order to maintain order and harmony within the Roman Empire. In the account of Josephus, we are informed about the earliest official edict of Claudius.[42] This edict was given because there arose a feud between Jews and Greeks in Alexandria. In this edict, we

---

From Paul to Valentinus, pp. 11-12. As mentioned above Lampe's work shows that Synagogues were dispersed and it was not centralized.

[38] For this view, see, Walters, "Romans, Jews, and Christians," p. 177. The openness to Gentiles characteristics and their ways of life endangered the exclusive boundaries of the Jewish ways of life and characteristics (cf. Philip Francis Esler, *Community and Gospel in Luke-Acts* (Cambridge: Cambridge University Press, 1987), p. 22.

[39] For an elaborate discussion see, Slingerland, *Claudian Policymaking*, pp. 151-168.

[40] Leonard Victor Rutgers, "Roman Policy toward the Jews: Expulsions from the City of Rome during the First Century C.E.," *Judaism and Christianity in First-Century Rome*, pp. 107-108.

[41] Elliott, *The Arrogance of Nations*, p. 98.

[42] Josephus, *Jewish Antiquities*, XIX. 285.2.

observe the restoration of special rights and the privileges of the Jews. The edict also warns both Jews and Greeks in Alexandria to maintain peaceful relations. He reprimands and threatens both parties with severe consequences if riots arise again. This warning provides the backdrop for understanding the significance of Suetonius' account (*Claudius* 25. 4). It is then possible that the edict of AD 49 was issued not because of Claudius' hatred for the Jews as a religious community, but that the unrest had a political liability. Emperor Claudius had to safeguard stability within the empire and suppress any unrest or disturbances. The measure was taken when the unrest among the members within the synagogues became constant and frequent and it attracted the attention of the larger population outside the synagogue. Emperor Claudius intervened as the unrest in the synagogues had the potential to spread unrest in the entire city and beyond. The Claudian edict did not expel the entire Jewish community, but only the key figures that were actively involved in the unrest. The edict impacted the Jews and the Jewish believers in Christ. It is also likely that a few Gentile sympathizers were expelled, though it cannot be proved from the text. However, the number of Gentiles expelled would not have been significant.[43]

[43] For elaborate discussions on the identity of *Chrestus*, scope and effect of expulsion refer to my work, *Acceptance Motif in Paul*, pp. 69-77.

i. Reading Romans within the Historical Context: The Impact of the Claudian Edict on the Believing Communities in Rome

The edict of Claudius expelling the Jews from Rome in AD 49 can be a possible historical background for Paul's letter to the Romans.[44] This edict could have significantly shaped the Christian faith in Rome in the early years.[45]

While there is evidence of the Jewish tradition in Rome in the first two centuries,[46] we cannot be sure of the degree of the influence of Jewish tradition within the Christian faith communities in Rome after its break from the synagogues. However, it is possible that because the synagogues were a worshipping place not only for the Jews, but also included proselytes, Greeks and God-fearers, who were, but a minority, the synagogue traditions likely shaped the Christian faith in Rome. In this regard, Edwin Broadhead proposes "Jewish Christianity exerts a strong influence upon Roman Christianity, even after the house churches and the synagogues seem to have separated."[47] Broadhead adds that the

---

[44] Those who take this view are A. Andrew Das, *Solving the Romans Debate* (Minneapolis: Fortress Press, 2007), pp. 149-202; C. E. B. Cranfield, *A Critical and Exegetical Commentary on the Epistle to the Romans*, I (ICC. Edinburgh: T&T Clark, 1975. pp. 17-18; Dunn, *Romans 1-8*, pp. xlix-liv; Fitzmyer, *Romans*, pp. 31-32; Philip Francis Esler, *Conflict and Identity in Romans: The Social Setting of Paul's Letter* (Minneapolis: Augsburg Fortress, 2003), pp. 98-108; Moo, *The Epistle to the Romans*, pp. 4-5. On the contrary, Sanday William and Arthus C. Headlam suggests that there was no expulsion under Claudius and that Dio's report stands valid against Suetonius or Acts (William Sanday and Arthur Headlam, *A Critical and Exegetical Commentary on the Epistle to the Romans*, ICC (New York: Charles Scribner's Sons 1901), p. xxl).

[45] Wiefel, "The Jewish Community in Ancient Rome," p. 92; Cranfield, *Romans*, I: p. 16.

[46] For evidence regarding Jewish teaching activity in Rome, refer to, Lampe, *From Paul to Valentinus*, p. 78, nt. 43.

[47] Edwin K. Broadhead, *Jewish ways of following Jesus: Redrawing the Religious Map of Antiquity*, WUNT 266 (Tübingen: Mohr Siebeck, 2010), p. 111. Broadhead uses terms like Christianity and Christian for Jewish and Gentile believers in Christ.

first Christians in Rome preserved and transmitted the cultivated traditions of Jewish teachings within the Christ believing circles, which also included the Gentile Christians.[48]

In the writings of Ambrosiaster, we get a glimpse of the tradition of Jewish activity in the Roman congregation.

> It is established that there were Jews living in Rome in the time of the apostles and that those Jews who had believed [in Christ] passed on to the Romans the tradition that they ought to profess Christ but keep the Law…One ought not to condemn the Romans, but to praise their faith because without seeing any of the signs or miracles, and without seeing any of the apostles, they nevertheless accepted faith in Christ, although in a Jewish manner.[49]

Another source that reflects the presence of Jewish tradition in the Roman Christ believing congregations is the anti-Marcionite prologue:

> The Romans lived in Italian territory. They were deceived by false prophets and under the name of our Lord Jesus Christ had been led astray to the Law and the Prophets. Writing to them from Corinth, the apostle recalls them to the true evangelical faith.[50]

From the witnesses from early sources it is reasonable to suggest that the Christian faith in Rome was influenced by Jewish ways of life, at least in its early years. However, the edict of Claudius also affected significantly in several areas the self-definitions of Christian faith as a group *vis-à-vis* Judaism.[51] James

---

[48] Broadhead, *Jewish ways of following Jesus*, p. 113.

[49] Cited by Raymond E. Brown & John P. Meier, *Antioch and Rome: New Testament Cradles of Catholic Christianity* (New York: Paulist, 1983), pp. 110-111.

[50] Cited by Werner Georg Kümmel, *The New Testament: The History of the Investigation of its Problems*, trans. S. McLean Gilmore & Howard C. Kee (Nashville: Abingdon Press, 1972 [German original, 1970]), p. 14.

[51] Walters assumes that the edict also provided a platform for the Jews to clarify their relation to Christians inorder to avoid censorship for disturbances

Walters provides a rationale for the shift in self-definitions among the Roman groups.

> The turmoil that Jewish Christians and God-fearing Gentiles experienced was compounded in the aftermath of the edict; not only were they separated from their "ethos," but they had at the same time to deal with the dissonance caused by changes in the Christian communities… The edict would have caused a considerable shift in roles of authority in the community… Gentile Christians, free from the scrupulous consciences of their law-abiding comrades, were no longer observing dietary laws and were not optimistic about renewing old practices… In Rome, because of the edict of Claudius and the growth of Gentile Christianity, those advocating freedom had the upper hand… The pressure that law-abiding Christians felt under these circumstances must have been enormous.[52]

This has an important bearing on our reading of Romans. First, with the Claudian edict, Christian faith in Rome took on a different phase; it broke away from the synagogue. This in turn might have affected its patterns of worship, at least concerning worship in the home-gatherings. Second, in the epistle to the Romans, which was written a few years after the event, we encounter a congregation of believers in Christ in Rome after the expulsion.[53] More significantly, it brought about a shift in the

---

caused by the Christians [James C. Walters, *Ethnic Issues in Paul's Letter to the Romans. Changing Self-Definitions in the Earliest Roman Christianity* (Pennsylvania: Trinity Press International, 1993), pp. 59-60]; Douglas Moo also shows that with the expulsion we find strong Gentile elements in the churches. Furthermore, Moo assumes that the decentralized nature of the Jewish community could also have contributed to several house churches [*The Epistle to the Romans*, p. 5]. However, one cannot be certain, for other factors probably could have been involved like the space available for meeting or the distance factor.

[52] Walters, *Ethnic Issues in Paul's Letter to the Romans*, p. 64.

[53] Wiefel, "The Jewish Community in Ancient Rome," p. 93.

composition of the home-gatherings,[54] which had become largely Gentile.[55] Third, since the Gentile believers in Christ were now a majority, leadership positions were also mainly in their hands. As the expelled members returned, they probably wanted to preserve their distinctive Jewish identity. This could have produced tension and divisions within the believing communities in Rome. In such a context Paul calls for acceptance of one another.

We note here that opinions differ on the audience of Romans. Some argue for the Jewish believers as a majority,[56] militating against the view that Paul was addressing mainly the Gentile believers.[57] There is no evidence to suggest a clear-cut division in terms of numbers. However, one thing is certain: both Jewish and Gentile believers are referred to in the epistle to the Romans.[58] A few evidences from the epistle that points to both the Jews and the Gentiles audience are the formula, "to the Jews first and also the Gentiles," is found frequently. There is also a redefinition of Jews and the reference to the Jews and the Gentiles praising God (Rom. 2-5; 15:8-12). The other instance where we find the presence of Jewish believers is in Romans 16:3-11, where Paul refers to

[54] The decentralized nature of the Jewish community from which the Christian community sprang would have contributed to the existence of several house churches (Moo, *Romans*, p. 5).

[55] Dunn, *Romans 1-8*, p. liii; Werner Georg Kümmel, *Introduction to the New Testament* ed. trans. by H. C. Kee (London: SCM Press, 1966), pp. 309-311.

[56] Ferdinand Christian Baur, *Paul the Apostle of Jesus Christ. His life and work, his epistles and his doctrine,* trans. Eduard Zeller, vol. I (1876, Reprint; Eugene, Oregon: Wipf and Stock Publishers, 2003), p. 321; T. Zahn, *Introduction to the New Testament* (Edinburgh: T&T Clark, 1909), I: p. 422.

[57] Sanday and Headlam, *Romans*, pp. xxi-xxiv; C. K. Barrett, *The Epistle to the Romans* (London: Adam and Charles Black, 1957), p. 22; Kümmel, *Introduction to the New Testament*, pp. 218-20; Das, *Solving the Romans Debate.*

[58] C. E. B. Cranfield points that it cannot be an overwhelming majority and a tiny minority (*Romans*, II: p. 21). A similar view is also held by Douglas Moo, *Romans*, p. 13; Sanday and Headlam suggest that the community to which Paul is writing is Gentile in its general complexion, but it also includes a subsequent number of Jews (*Romans*, p. xxxiv); Joseph Fitzmyer also proposes a mixed community of both Jews and the Gentiles, but predominantly of Gentile background (*Romans*, p. 33).

Aquila and Priscilla, Andronicus, Junia, and Herodian. Paul also addresses the Jews (Rom. 2:3, 17) and his readers with the Mosaic Law (Rom. 6:14; 7:1, 4); refer to Abraham as our ancestor (Rom. 14:1) and to issues surrounding Jewish people (Rom. 3:19-20, 27-31; 4:12-15; 5:13-14; 6:14; 7:1-25; 8:2-4; 9:30-10:8). Similarly, there are also references to Gentile believers in the epistle. Paul refers to himself as an apostle to the Gentiles (Rom. 1:5-6; 15:14-21), even his arguments about God's plan for Jews in Romans 11:1-24 is directed to Gentiles in 11:13 and his exhortations on dietary laws and observance of special days were directed to both the Jews and the Gentiles (Rom. 14-15). This indicates that Paul was aware of the people groups among the believers in Rome and his teachings in Romans were directed to all. The vulnerability of the returning Jews makes Paul warns his Gentile audience against the attitude of superiority (Rom. 11:17-21). In his exhortation on the "weak" and the "strong" in Romans 14:1-15:6, Paul also encourages the "strong" to accept the "weak", most of who were returnees from the expulsion. Thus, it is reasonable to conclude that with the expulsion of the Jews and the Jewish believers in Christ, Gentile believers would have increased in number, and by the time Paul was writing Romans, Gentiles could have been in majority even when the Jewish believers returned. When the expelled Jewish believers in Christ returned, they must also have wanted to uphold their distinct Jewish identity, which produced tension and conflicts, dividing the members of the faith community. Thus, Paul reminds them of their new identity in Christ in Romans 1-11, and from Romans 12-13 he speaks of attitudes and beliefs necessary for this new identity, which further leads to harmonious living in Romans 14-15.

Having situated Romans within the historical setting of the Claudian Edict, the task that remains is to explore the privileges and status in Roman society as it has bearings on Paul's exhortation in Romans 12-13.

Social Status within the Roman Society

Roman society was a stratified society in which privileges and status played an important role. An individual's place within the society was also connected to honor-shame nexus. This section will highlight the privileged and public personality in Roman society, and the patronage system linked to the honor-shame nexus.

i. The Privileged and Public Personality in Roman Society

The Roman law divided the society into higher and lower status, i.e., the *honestiores* and *humiliores*.[59] There were "orders" which were social categories defined by the state. It involved statutory or customary rules. During the time of emperor Augustus, he re-introduced the Republican system of orders, i.e., *ordo* and rank. The privileged group could be identified based on "publicly recognized or recognizable criteria."[60] Thus, Roman society defined the place of its citizens and strangers by rank and status.

The Senatorial orders were the highest and a prestigious order and its membership was based on high birth by traditional standards, wealth, and moral excellence. Of course, the last criterion is questionable as it was not strictly kept and evaluated by the elite. The Senatorial household up to the third generation enjoyed special privileges in public as well as in private affairs.[61] The Senatorial order was an exclusive group and they possessed legal position, social privilege, and political prominence. They were protected from harsh penalties, in the capital and non-capital

---

[59] For further reference to the terms refer to Peter Garnsey, *Social Status and Legal Privilege in the Roman Empire* (Oxford: Clarendon Press, 1970), pp. 221-222.

[60] Garnsey, *Social Status and Legal Privilege in the Roman Empire*, p. 235. Peter Garnsey & Richard Saller, *The Roman Empire: Economy, Society and Culture* (California: University of California Press, 2015), p. 136. On the rank and social status in Rome, see also Bruce Winter, "Roman Law and Society in Romans 12-15," in Peter Oakes (ed.) *Rome in the Bible and the Early Church* (Carlisle, Cumbria: Paternoster Press, 2002), pp. 76-77.

[61] Garnsey & Saller, *The Roman Empire*, p. 136.

cases. This protection was because of their privilege of trial before the Roman Senate. The political supremacy of the Senate in the Republican tradition can be reflected in the administration and the discharge of the law. Thus, during the time of emperor Augustus social superiority of this group was maintained by forbidding marriage between male senators and freedwomen and women of senatorial rank and freedman or those with low connections.[62]

Next to the senatorial household and order was the equestrian order. The members of the *equites Romani* also enjoyed the special social status. The equestrians resembled the senatorial in the criteria for members like high birth and wealth, but in the second degree. Its members were characterized by an aristocratic ethos. This was a wealthy group and senatorial ranks were filled from the class of *equites*. Among the equestrians there was the distinguished group belonging to the imperial elite and based in Rome.[63]

The next in the aristocratic order were the decurions and the councilors of towns and cities who were members of the local council within the Roman Empire. Their privileges were comparable with the Senators in Rome. They were considered as privileged aristocracy. Respectable birth, social background, wealth, and good moral standing also defined their membership. However, their criterion was to a degree below the equestrians.[64] Dishonorable profession or a criminal record barred a person from becoming a member of the order of decurions. Free birth was a requirement to be a Decurion. A freedman rarely could be a member, however, even if he could win a membership because of financial position, he/she could only enjoy special benefits and not as full members of the order. In the cities the privileges of the decurions were comparable with the senators in Rome. The

---

[62] Garnsey, *Social Status and Legal Privilege in the Roman Empire*, pp. 236-237.

[63] Garnsey & Saller, *The Roman Empire*, pp. 136-137.

[64] Garnsey & Saller, *The Roman Empire*, p. 137.

financial well-being and the development of the cities depended on the decurions.[65]

The senators, the equestrians and the decurions were the three elite groups comprising of a small number of the population of the Roman Empire. Generally, men in a Roman society dominated the public arena, whereas women were mainly confined within the private sphere and activities. Women were identified by her family affiliations. Nonetheless, women within the elite group, i.e., the mother and also the wife of the Roman emperors and senators played an important part over their son's and husband's leadership and decisions. An example we find in ancient Rome is Livia Drusilla Augusta, the wife of Augustus Caesar who was a companion and an advisor to her husband. Also Aurelia, mother of Gaius Julius Caesar had an immense influence on the leadership of her son. Generally, women belonging to the elite group and the wealthy working class had access to formal education.[66]

Below the elite group was the Plebeians, the free average-working citizens of Rome. The Plebs were mainly lower working class, but some plebeians who were doing well had made for themselves a place among the high social levels and joined the equestrian class. There were official and non-official plebs. The official plebs enjoyed the benefits of higher social status.[67] Some freedmen were given the opportunity for some form of religious connection with the emperor. This is evident during the time of emperor Augustus, who allowed freedmen to become priests of the imperial cult.[68]

---

[65] Garnsey, *Social Status and Legal Privilege in the Roman Empire*, pp. 242-243.

[66] Joy Mosier-Dubinsky, "Women in Ancient Rome," *JCCC Honors Journal*, 4/2 (2013). https://scholarspace.jccc.edu/cgi/viewcontent.cgi?article=1040&context=honors_journal (accessed on May 6, 2020).

[67] Bruce Winter, "Roman Law and Society in Romans 12-15," pp. 76-77.

[68] On priests in the imperial cult see D. Fishwick, *The Imperial Cult in the Latin West. Studies in the Ruler Cult of the Western Provinces of the Roman Empire*, vol. 3 (Leiden & Boston: Brill, 2002).

At the bottom of the Roman society were the slaves. The slaves contributed to the majority of the workforce and they comprised of the larger section of Roman society. The slaves in the Roman law were classified as "speaking tools" (*instrumentum vocale*) and they were at the mercy and the disposal of the master.[69] Other laborers were "free tenants," but many of them experienced severe exploitation because of their economic situation and lack of power. The landless laborers who possessed freedom and citizenship also had to bear the pressures from their oppressive landlords. Peasants with land were independent, but were burdened with taxes and army service. Thus, the heavy taxation and the demands for services in the army and social services made the individuals and groups from the lower strata of the Roman society to look and seek for rural patronage.[70]

In general, Roman culture and society were very conscious of rank and social status. Therefore, Roman society took great care in identifying the social status and legal privileges and priorities of the elite group. The privileged group enjoyed legal privileges. The source of legal privilege was honor and prestige, which in Roman society was *dignitas*. *Dignitas* depended on political position, influence, and wealth. In the administration of the law by the Roman judicial system discrimination in favor of citizens was also practiced. In any crime or misdeed, citizens of the Roman Empire received a milder penalty, then foreigners or slaves for the same offense.[71] The status was also visible in their clothing. The identity of the senators was also visible in their dress code, i.e., they wore the toga with the broad purple stripe on the tunic (*latus clavus*). This dress code was restricted to senators and their sons. The gold ring on the finger and the narrow purple strips on their toga identified the equestrians.[72]

---

[69] Garnsey & Saller, *The Roman Empire*, p. 139.

[70] Garnsey & Saller, *The Roman Empire*, pp. 135-136.

[71] Garnsey, *Social Status and Legal Privilege in the Roman Empire*, pp. 258-262.

[72] Refer to Winter, "Roman Law and Society in Romans 12-15," pp. 76-77; Garnsey & Saller, *The Roman Empire*, p. 139.

The social ranking was also important in the public appearance, especially in the theatre, amphitheater, and circus. They could also dine at public expense and were bestowed with more gifts than the general citizens. The visibility of status consciousness was primarily seen in two areas of social life, i.e., in the theatres and the public banquets and private dinners. First, in Rome going to the theater was popular among all classes of people. Entertainments especially through comedy influenced and impacted the social patterns of life. The privileged group, i.e., those belonging to the higher social standing in the Roman society occupied special seats that were assigned according to social ranks. Second, banquets and dinners both public and private were common affairs in Rome. This is another arena of social life where the practice of class distinction is visible. Social hierarchy was strictly maintained in public banquets with the serving of food according to the social ranks in descending order. This practice was also followed in private dinners in the quality and quantity of food served and also in the seating arrangements.[73] Linked to the status is also wealth. This was displayed in the lifestyle of the elite group. The Roman historian Seneca illustrates it in Ep. 27. 5-8. Wealth and status were displayed also in a beautiful mansion and numerous educated slaves.[74]

The differences in social status occasionally resulted in tensions and envy among the elite groups or between members belonging to different social statuses. For example, we read about the resentment among senators at the over-exercise of power by Sejanus who was Tiberius' praetorian prefect and a man of the second rank.[75] The conflicts could even end up in the civil law courts. If it did, the judge and the jury were required to pronounce judgment and when this happens, it results in the public humiliation of the opponents. In a context where the system of honor and shame was closely observed the public shame against

---

[73] On the social rank and status in theatres and public and private dinners, see Winter, "Roman Law and Society in Romans 12-15," pp. 77-78.

[74] Garnsey & Saller, *The Roman Empire*, p. 143.

[75] Garnsey & Saller, *The Roman Empire*, p. 141.

whom the judgment was pronounced was most hurting.[76] Thus, in the Roman social hierarchy based on status, wealth, position, and birth were extensively maintained both in public and private spheres of life and gathering. Connected to the social status was the patronage system that was widely practiced.

ii. Patronage

The Roman Empire was tied together through a network of patronage. A good emperor was also expected to be a patron and a benefactor. The emperor and his household occupied the highest place in the social structure, thus as the benefactor, his subjects could only repay the imperial benefaction through respect and loyalty. Seneca mentions that the emperor who had been a great patron to his subjects did not require personal guards to protect him because his benefits protected him (*De Clementia* 1.13.5). The emperor could either give away his benefits individually or to favored groups like the Roman plebs and the army. Those in close association with the emperor had access to the privileged circles. They also had access to benefits from offices, financial assistance, or even citizenship for foreigners. These benefits were treated as the emperor's benefits. In return the beneficiaries were to display devoted service and gratitude to the emperor. The emperor in Rome did not only practice patron-client bonds, but it extended to provinces outside Rome. Roman provincial Governors' and other officials had a patronal role. The provincial governors in their capacity could help secure citizenship, offices, and honor from Rome. They also could show favor on administrative and legal decisions. In return, the governors received gifts and support from grateful provincials.[77] The patronage system indirectly is also connected to the imperial cult in Rome and the local imperial

---

[76] Winter, "Roman Law and Society in Romans 12-15," pp. 79-80. On public shame and humiliation see Robert A. Kaster, "The Shame of the Romans," *Transactions of the American Philological Associations*, vol. 127 (1997), pp. 1-19.

[77] On superior or inferior services, especially the emperor as the patron and benefactor, refer to, Garnsey & Saller, *The Roman Empire*, pp. 174-176.

cults. The provincial and urban elites sponsored the imperial cult to win the favor of Rome and this practice was associated as a diplomatic connection to the emperor. Thus, the emperor cult also became a means of political and religious expression of solidarity with the Roman Empire outside Rome, in the cities and the Roman provinces.[78]

In Roman society the patronage system was an important form of social relations among the elites.[79] Through this network the elites and other wealthy personalities who had personal relations with the emperor and the imperial household maintained their wealth and prominence in cities. The local elites on securing a position through their connections with the emperor and the imperial court generated power and wealth to interfere and take control of the affairs of the cities where they belonged. Wealthy and local elites also became patrons of local artisans and the local community.[80] The patronage system aimed to enhance the power and status of the elite as it was connected to the exchange of benefits and obligations. The patrons expected a return from the client for the benefit given by the patron. The local elites in return were honored by the beneficence. Their names were honored and their birthdays celebrated in the localities and the cities. This system also indicated the inferior status of the client with the patron. The status of a patron was also measured and elevated by the number of clients attached to the patron. On the part of the client, one also looked for worthy and wealthy patrons, someone who was reliable and could be of help. Patronal relations benefitted both the patron and the client, especially among the elite classes as it established

[78] Simon R. F., *Price, Rituals and Poor: The Roman Imperial Cult in Asia Minor* (Cambridge: Cambridge University Press, 1984), 57-69. Efrain Agosto, "Patronage and Commendation, Imperial and Anti-imperial," *Paul and the Roman Imperial Order*, Edited by Richard A. Horsely (London: Trinity Press International, 2004), p. 104.

[79] Garnsey & Saller, *The Roman Empire*, p. 96.

[80] Richard A. Horsely, *Paul and the Roman Imperial Order*, p. 15.

the status and reputation of both the patron and the client.[81] The status of the patron was enhanced and greatly honored by the beneficence. Thus, the honor-shame system was connected to the networking of patronage.

iii. Honor and Reciprocity Ethic in Greco-Roman Society

The cultural values of honor and shame were pivotal in the Mediterranean world.[82] Bruce J. Malina describes honor "as socially proper attitudes and behavior" that is bound up in the symbols and intersections of power, sexual status, and religion. Malina goes on to explain that honor is a claim to the worth of oneself and the social acknowledgment of that worth. In such a context an individual examines their actions within the societal norms of what is meaningful and valuable.[83] Thus, to honor a person is to acknowledge that the person's behavior and action are as per the societal norms.

The honor can be ascribed or acquired. Ascribed honor is related to the family. It is inherited. Being born into an honorable family provides one with status and honor. A person in power can also ascribe it. Acquired honor refers to the socially claimed worth of a person. A person's actions is examined in light of the societal norms. A person acquires his/her worth through social interactions and social patterns that excel over others in the group, community, or society. In acquired honor challenge and response are constantly at play. Malina rightly identifies three phases of interactions of challenge-response in the context of honor. First, the challenge that involves some action on the part of the challenger. Second, the perception of the message to the directed individual and the

---

[81] Efrain Agosto, "Patronage and Commendation, Imperial and Anti-imperial," pp. 104-105.

[82] Zeba Crook, "Honor, shame and social status Revisited," *Journal of Biblical Literature,* 128/3 (2009): p. 591. For details, see also Carlin Barton, *Roman Honor: The Fire in the Bones* (Berkeley: University of California Press, 2001).

[83] Bruce J. Malina, *The New Testament World: Insights from Cultural Anthropology* (1981, London: SCM press, 1983), pp. 27-28.

public. Third, the reaction of the individual at the receiving end and the evaluation of the reaction by the public. The challenge can be either positive or negative. A positive claim can help an individual to enter the social space of another and it is mutually beneficial. A negative claim can remove an individual from his/her social space temporarily or permanently.[84] Thus, in the first-century Mediterranean world the interactions at the societal or community level were considered an attempt to acquire honor from the community or even within the context of social equals.

The system of honor was widely operated in the Greco-Roman society. An individual was recognized in the society or a group, and their place was determined either by honor or shame they received within the social standards. The honor was not only desired by the rich and powerful, but by all individuals. Any individual could make claims to honor, however, its recognition was according to the standards within the community. For example, the graffiti on the remains of Pompeii portray two men competing for honor from their readers.[85] The Roman law as well as their social law and cultural setting were constructed based on their social rights and privileges. An individual with superior status or a high-ranking person in the Roman system had special legal privileges and protections.[86]

In Roman society an individual or the community owed their benefactor gratitude and reciprocity in either material good or by giving respect and honor. In Roman society, the morality of obligation can be seen in the exposition of terms like *officium* (duty) and *beneficium* (gift-giving). Some texts highlight the ethic of reciprocity involving the interchange of the acts of kindness, which is an important principle of obligation (Cicero, *De Officiis*

---

[84] For the discussion on ascribed and acquired honor refer to Malina, *The New Testament World*, pp. 29-30.

[85] Peter Oakes, *Reading Romans in Pompeii* (Minneapolis: Fortress Press, 2009), p. 33. Refer also to Halvor Moxnes, "Honor and Righteousness in Rome," *JSNT* 32 (1988): p. 63.

[86] Refer to, Garnsey, *Social Status and Legal Privilege in the Roman Empire*; Winter, "Roman Law and Society in Romans 12-15," pp. 67-68.

1. 20-23).[87] Likewise, others emphasize obligation and gift-giving, where a return service becomes obligatory after an initial gift was received (Seneca, *De Beneficiis* 1.1.8-10).[88] Apart from such exchange in the context of goods and services, relationships of obligations also existed on an interpersonal level, where one is indebted either in service or in relating to another individual and their social surroundings (Cicero, *De Officiis* 1. 33, 41).[89] Ingratitude was severely dealt with in Roman society. Seneca claims ingratitude as the worst of the vices that harms society. He identifies a series of moral evils that harm the society like homicide, tyrants, thieves, adulterers, traitors and concludes that of all these the worst is the ingratitude in a person.[90] Peter Garnsey also asserts "favor or service gave rise to a social relationship between Romans."[91] Garnsey's view, especially applies to a society where patron and benefaction involves the ethic of honor and status.

The Honor System was also connected to the practice of gift-giving that was common in the ancient Mediterranean world. The practice of the exchange of gifts is a universal phenomenon indicating the sense of obligation that prevailed in ancient and modern societies. Marcel Mauss identifies the exchange of gifts as a universal phenomenon that calls for a sense of obligation. Mauss claims that in the ancient societies exchange of gifts involved the nature of reciprocity involving individuals and groups and this act of giving and receiving established social relations.[92] This practice is exercised both in the public and the private realm. Within the public realm was the practice of civic *euergetism* or benefaction,

---

[87] M. Tullius Cicero, *De Officiis*, Edited by Walter Miller. http://www.perseus.tufts.edu (accessed on February 11, 2020).

[88] Seneca, *De Beneficiis*, www.Perseus.tufts.edu (accessed on February 11, 2020).

[89] Cicero, *De Officiis*. http://www.perseus.tufts.edu.

[90] Seneca, *De Beneficiis*, www.Perseus.tufts.edu.

[91] Garnsey & Saller, *The Roman Empire*, p. 174.

[92] Marcel Mauss, *The Gift: The Form and Reason of Exchange in Archaic Societies* (London: Free Press, 1954), pp. 10-12.

which was a Greek system that was inducted into Roman society. In this system the nobles or the Roman aristocrats gave their wealth towards public building and civil institutions like roads, temples, health care, public buildings, or public entertainment. In return public bestowal of honor was expected and called for.[93] The other social system connected to gift-giving was the patronage system that was commonly practiced in Roman society. In this practice those from the upper strata of society would develop a patron-client relationship with those from the lower strata of the society. The patron provided security and physical protection, material goods, financial aid, legal support, and other services in exchange for honor from the client.[94] Thus, it is clear that the practice of gift-giving invited reciprocity. John Barclay observes that the exchange of gifts encouraged social bonding and also recognized another person inviting a "personal, enduring and reciprocal relationship" also indicates the reciprocity in connection to gift-giving.[95] In the Roman society members of equal social standing could exchange compatible benefits and gifts. However, the majority of the social relation was built on the high or low social standing where expectations were superior or inferior services. The recipient was expected to acknowledge and make known the benefactor's generosity and power.

Within the context in which the values of honor and shame were widely regarded and practiced, in Roman society we also find instances when status and honor were challenged, for instance, when the social inferiors insulted respectable citizens. Such instances could even be in the case of the emperor who fell

---

[93] See, John H. Elliott, "Patronage and Clientage," *The Social Sciences and New Testament Interpretation*, Edited by *Richard* Rohrbaugh (Peabody, MA: Hendrickson, 1996), p. 151; John Barclay, *Paul and the Gift* (Grand Rapids, MI: William B. Eerdmans, 2015), pp. 33-35; Spencer Elliott, "Political Paul and the Social Context of Romans 12-13," pp. 4-5. https://www.academia.edu (accessed on August 13, 2019).

[94] See, Elliott, "Patronage and Clientage," pp. 148-149.

[95] Barclay, *Paul and the Gift*, p. 31.

short of the public expectations. One such instance is described by Cornelius Tacitus in *The Annals* 12:43[96] that mention:

> Several prodigies occurred in that year. Birds of evil omen perched on the Capitol; houses were thrown down by frequent shocks of earthquake, and as the panic spread, all the weak were trodden down in the hurry and confusion of the crowd. Scanty crops too and consequent famine were regarded as a token of calamity. Nor were there merely whispered complaints; while Claudius was administering justice, the populace crowded round him with a boisterous clamor and drove him to a corner of the forum, where they violently pressed on him till he broke through the furious mob with a body of soldiers. It was ascertained that Rome had provision for no more than fifteen days and it was through the signal bounty of heaven and the mildness of the winter that its desperate plight was relieved. And yet in the past days Italy used to send supplies for the legions into distant provinces, and even now it is not a barren soil, which causes distress. But, we prefer to cultivate Africa and Egypt and trust the life of the Roman people to ships and all their risks.

Orosius also refers to this famine, which affected the whole of Syria, and places it in the fourth year of the reign of Claudius.[97] Thus, we see that during the reign of Claudius poor harvest had resulted in a shortage of grain and the people responded violently by trying to attack Claudius. He escaped the attack by the mob, but took steps to import food for the survival of that winter. In such instances the status and identity of a person did not matter to those affected by the calamity or circumstances. Such incidents also revealed the weakness of those in power. Jon E. Lendon remarks, "Insult also argued weakness, the inability to defend honor."[98]

---

[96] Cornelius Tacitus in *The Annals* 12:43 http://www.perseus.tufts.edu/hopper/text?doc=Perseus%3Atext%3A1999.02.0078%3Abook%3D12%3Achapter%3D43 (accessed on April 10, 2020).

[97] Paulus Orosius, *History Against the Pagans*. 7:6. https://b-ok.cc/book/2918708/c67cc4 (accessed on April 10, 2020).

[98] Jon E. Lendon, *Empire of Honour: The Art of Government in the Roman World* (Oxford: Oxford University Press, 1997), p. 51.

iv. Impact on Paul

The honor and shame system that was widely practiced in Roman society is also reflected in Pauline Epistles. In the Epistle to the Romans in his defense of the gospel Paul proclaims, "I am not ashamed of the gospel" (Rom 1:16). Paul's gospel is about the Messiah who was crucified on the cross and Paul had to defend the power of the gospel about the crucified Messiah. From the Greco-Roman honor-shame system, it would have been a shame to preach the gospel about a crucified person. Thus, Paul says he is not ashamed of the gospel as a rejection of the honor-shame definition that prevailed among the elites in Roman society.[99] Neill Elliott argues convincingly that throughout the epistle to the Romans one encounters ideological tensions. However, unlike those who argue that Romans is Paul's political critique and the war on the Roman imperial order, Elliott rightly points out that Romans does not provide a "direct critique of empire."[100] Romans provide us with theological arguments directed to faith and salvation of the believers in Christ, the priority of the Jews and the salvific place of the Jews and the non-Jews, and the judgment upon Jews and non-Jews. The epistle to the Romans is Paul's exhortation towards building and maintaining cordial relationships among the believers in Christ and also within the larger society especially the Roman imperial context. This is argued in this study.

Summary

From our analysis of the historical context of Romans we can thus sum up:

First, the early Christians in Rome worshiped together with the Jews and a few Gentile sympathizers in the synagogues. However, the dissensions between the Jews and the believers in Christ in the synagogues attracted the attention of the Roman authority resulting in the Claudian edict of expulsion in AD 49.

---

[99] Robert Jewett and Roy David Kotansky, *Romans: A Commentary*, ed. Eldon Jay Epp, Hermeneia - a Critical and Historical Commentary on the Bible (Minneapolis, MN: Fortress Press, 2006), pp. 136-139.

[100] Elliott, *The Arrogance of the Nations*, p. 61.

One permanent result of this expulsion was that believers in Christ and Jews parted ways, giving rise to the home-gatherings of the believers in Christ.

Second, Roman society was a stratified society in which class and status played an important role in defining the place of an individual and family. Connected to the rank and social status was the patronage system and linked to this system was the honor and reciprocity ethic.

Thus, within the context of the privileges and the powers in the Roman law, the next chapter will interpret the instructions of Paul in Romans 12-13. While Paul's writings may be interpreted as directed to Roman ideologies and establishments and authorities, I want to argue that Paul was primarily concerned with the implications of some aspects of Roman law for Christian discipleship to which we now turn.

Chapter 3

Romans 12-13 and the Roman Social Status

There are indications of imperial ideologies in Romans 12-13 and it is reflected in Paul's exhortation to the believers in Christ. The notion that believers belong to the wider Roman imperial surrounding and participate in the public and private spheres is evident in Romans. Thus, in this chapter, we will focus on Paul's gospel in Romans 12-13 and the Roman social status.

Interpretations of Romans 12-13

In recent years there have been several studies that focus on reading Paul within the context of the Roman Empire.[101] However,

[101] A few that I have had access are, Elliott, *The Arrogance of the Nations*; Idem, *Liberating Paul: The Justice of God and the Politics of the Apostle* (Sheffield: Sheffield Academic Press, 1995); Richard A. Horsley (ed), *Paul and the Roman Imperial Order* (Harrisburgh, PA: Trinity Press International, 2004); Idem, *Paul and Empire: Religion and Power in Roman Imperial Society* (Harrisburgh, PA: Trinity Press International, 1997); Esler, *Conflict and Identity in Romans;* J. Paul Sampley, *Paul in the Greco: Roman World: A Handbook* (Harrisburg, PA: Trinity Press International, 2003); Jacob Taubes, *The Political Theology of Paul*, Translated by Dana Hollander (1993; Stanford:

even before the recent studies on reading Paul within the context of the imperial ideology, Adolf Deissmann in *Light from the Ancient East* demonstrates the presence of imperial ideology in Paul's epistles and refers to it as "a silent protest."[102] Deissmann observed the distinct and overlapping titles used for God in the first century among Romans, Greeks, Jews, and Christians.[103] Yet, today scholars are not assuming "a silent protest," but are obvious in pointing to the political Roman ideologies and languages, anti/counter-imperial overtones in Paul's texts.[104] These works read Paul and his gospel about Christ in the context of imperial ideology. Along this line, we also observe the reading of Romans 12-13. For example, Sylvia C. Keesmat emphasizes reading Romans 12-13 as a political manifesto against the Roman establishment.[105] While I acknowledge that there are teachings directed to the Roman establishment, but the problem with Keesmat's interpretation lies in the view that Paul's primary focus and manifesto in Romans 12-13 is rooted in the Roman establishment. By this I do not undermine the presence of the Roman establishment in reading Paul and the New Testament.

Warren Carter responds by proposing the establishment of alternative communities. Carter maintains that in the Roman world, one does not find opportunities to intervene in the political process, neither do we find opportunities to form political parties, to sign

---

Stanford University Press, 2004); Dieter Georgi, *Theocracy in Paul's Praxis and Theology* (Minneapolis: Fortress Press, 1991); Elliott, "Political Paul and the Social Context of Romans 12-13."

[102] Adolf Deissmann, *Light from the Ancient East: The New Testament Illustrated by Recently discovered Texts of the Graeco-Roman World* (trans. L. R. M. Strachan, 2nd edn; London: Hodder & Stoughton, 1927), pp. 242-278, the quotation from p. 259.

[103] Deissmann, *Light from the Ancient East*, pp. 347-350.

[104] D. C. Lopez, *Apostle to the Conquered: Reimagining Paul's Mission* (Minneapolis, MN: Fortress Press, 2008), p. 8.

[105] Sylvia C. Keesmat, "If your enemy is hungry: Love and subversive politics in Romans 12-13," Robert L. Brawley (ed) *Character and Ethics and the New Testament: Moral Dimensions of Scripture* (Louisville: John Knox Press, 2007), pp. 141-158.

petitions, or organize reform mass movements. The reason is that the elite groups were strong and would not easily surrender their wealth and power. Hence, Carter believes that the texts of the New Testament emphasize forming alternative communities that can provide life-giving alternatives to the ways of the empire. Carter takes an example from Paul's epistle to the Romans and urges the Roman believers in Christ, not to be conformed to the world, but to be transformed by the renewing of minds (Rom. 12:2). Carter also goes on to point that Paul's exhortation in Romans 12 is to urge the believers to form communities of mutual support, loving one another, and not being haughty but practicing hospitality. Carter stresses the need for alternative communities that differ from "the indebtedness and dependency of patron-client relations, from the empire's hierarchy and domination, and the execution of military retaliation. They produce a very different societal experience and very different ways of being human."[106] The need for alternative communities is a welcoming response to the reality of the Roman establishment and ideology in the Pauline writings. Nevertheless, I agree with Spencer Elliott[107] that the proposal for alternative communities should not be overemphasized to give the impression that the communities were established specifically as alternatives to Roman establishments and we forget the larger oppositions to the communities of the Mediterranean world. Still, Carter's hypothesis for alternative communities of mutual support and love in Romans can be considered as we interpret Romans 12-13.

The over-emphasis on Paul and the imperial system or the interpretation of Paul within the imperial ideology as the primary purpose of Paul's message in Romans or even in Romans 12-13 can result in a bias interpretation of Paul's ethical instructions. To this, John Barclay proposes that Paul is referring to a broader anti-God power in the world.[108] However, instead of a general

---

[106] Warren Carter, *The Roman Empire and the New Testament: An Essential guide* (Nashville: Abingdon, 2006), pp. 20-21.

[107] Elliott, "Political Paul and the Social Context of Romans 12-13," p. 2.

[108] Barclay, *Paul and the Gift*, pp. 383-387.

reference, Spencer Elliott rightly asserts that the political implications of Paul's ethical instructions come as an effect of his instruction against the broader culture. Hence the political force of Paul's message should not be taken as a primary function. The way Paul framed the life of the community by modifying the system that existed during his time include political implications.[109] Likewise, for Bruce Winter, Paul in Romans 12-13 is evaluating and interacting with the cultural values from the standpoint of the privileges and powers in the Roman law. Winter points out that Paul in the ethical instructions in Romans identifies the importance of the "will of God," over against privileges and powers that determined the relationship between social superiors and inferiors. He elaborates that Paul's appeal in Romans 9-11 is not on the conduct grounded on privilege, but on the "mercies of God." This, according to Winter is indicated further with the use of the Greek conjunction *oun* (οὐν), which means "therefore" in opening Romans 12:1. Believers in Rome must form their conduct based on the mercies of God and it should also guide them in their approach to the relationship between Jewish and Gentile believers in Rome.[110]

Thus, taking into account the community of the believers in Christ in relating to the wider Roman society within the context of multiple identities and roles we will briefly look into three spheres of the believer's life in Romans 12-13: the individual sphere (12:1-2), the community sphere (12:3-13), and the social and civil sphere (12:14-21; 13:1-10).

The Individual Sphere: Living, Holy and Well-Pleasing (Romans 12:1-2)

Interpreters of Romans agree that Paul's exhortation to the individual believers in Romans 12:1-2 sets the tone of Paul's ethical teachings for the entire parenetic section in Romans 12-

---

[109] Elliott, "Political Paul and the Social Context of Romans 12-13," pp. 2-3.

[110] Bruce Winter, "Roman Law and Society in Romans 12-15," pp. 68-69.

15:13.[111] Here Paul makes a personal address by exhorting the believers concerning life acceptable to God, especially in their personal relationship with God as His children.

i. The Mercy of Liberation (Romans 12:1a)

Paul begins by beseeching the believers in Christ through the mercies of God. The Greek word *oiktirmōn* (οἰκτιρμῶν) is used for mercy, instead of the more general Greek word *eleos*. The noun form *oiktirmōs* occurs twice in Paul, in Romans 12:1 and in 2 Corinthians 1:3, and both occurrences it refers to God's mercy. The notion of the mercy of God surfaces explicitly and implicitly in Romans 1-11, especially the two key texts are Romans 3:21-26 and Romans 9:14-16. In Romans 3:21-26 the emphasis is on the righteousness of God that is manifested in His redemption and mercy. So also, in Romans 9-11 Paul's exhortation is centered on the faithful fulfillment of God's promise in showing mercy to the people. The mercy of God that Paul calls for, is a mercy of liberation, a liberation of the physical body from the bondage of sin, and for reclaiming the body as a sacrifice worthy before God (Rom. 12:1). Through the mercy of God the believers are liberated from the bondage and their bodies are a sacrifice representing true worship.[112]

ii. Transformation and Renewal (Romans 12:2a)

From the freedom and liberation of the body as reclaimed for God in Romans 12:1, Paul moves to the notion of transformation and renewal in Romans 12:2. Robert Jewett brings the connection

[111] Ernst Käsemann asserts that Romans 12:1-2 provide the main theme [*Commentary on Romans*, Trans. G.W. Bromiley (Grand Rapids: Eerdmans, 1980), p. 323]; C.E.B. Cranfield takes the two verses as the introduction to the whole section [*A Critical and Exegetical Commentary on the Epistle to the Romans* (ICC; 2 vols; Edinburgh: Clark, 1979), 2. p. 595]; while for James D. G. Dunn it is the summary of the whole section [*Romans 9-16*, vol. 38b (WBC; Dallas: Word, 1988), p. 707].

[112] Nijay K. Gupta, "What 'Mercies of God'? Oiktrimos in Romans 12:1 against its Septuagintal Background," *Bulletin for Biblical Research*, 22/1 (2012), pp. 93-94.

between Romans 12:1 and Romans 12:2. Jewett rightly observes that in Romans 12:1 there are "somatic relations," while in Romans 12:2 the concentration is on "mental outlook."[113] In Romans 12:2 with the use of the Greek words *suschēmatizesthe* (συσχηματίζεσθε) meaning conformed and *metamorphousthe* (μεταμορφοῦσθε) meaning transformed. Paul employs the first word in a negative setting with the "world" by exhorting the believers not to be conformed by this age, but to be transformed by renewing their minds according to the good and well-pleasing will of God. "Do not be conformed to this age" in Romans 12:2 indicates the recognition of power and forces at play in the present world/age. Paul perceives the effect and power of social values, norms, cultural ethos, ethnic and social groups, and institutions like imperial values and norms that dictate and build individual attitudes and behaviors.[114] Some interpreters also interpret it as not conforming to sinful ways of life.[115] Spiritual renewal and transformation begin with an individual member, it is supposed to take root in an individual's inner being as Paul says by the "renewing of the mind."

The Greek word *anakainōsei* (ἀνακαινώσει) is made up of *ana* which means up or completing a process and *kainōs* meaning fresh, new, or renewal. Thus, *anakainōsei* means becoming new and different, a new development or renewal (cf. Col. 3:1; Eph. 4:23). The verb "renew" in the present tense suggests a continuing renewal or ongoing sanctification.[116] The entire clause reads "but be transformed by the renewing of the mind" (Rom. 12:2). It is a

---

[113] Jewett, *Romans: A Commentary*, p. 731.

[114] Dunn, *Romans 9-16*, p. 712.

[115] L. Wilhoit Ryken & Longmann III, Dictionary *of Biblical Imagery: An Encyclopedic exploration of the Images, Symbols, Motifs, Metaphors, Figures of Speech and Literary Patterns of the Bible* (Illinois: InterVarsity Press, 1998), p. 759.

[116] G. E. Ladd, *A Theology of the New Testament* (Grand Rapids, MI: William B. Eerdmans, 1974), p. 476; J. Murry, *The Epistle to the Romans* (NICNT; Grand Rapids, MI: William B. Eedrmans, 1975), p. 114; Leon Morris, *The Epistle to the Romans* (Grand Rapids, MI: William B. Eerdmans, 1988), p. 435.

call to allow God to change one's inner being continually and not just a one-time event. The use of "mind" is a reference to human beings within the context of "the inner direction of his/*her* thought and will and the orientation of his/*her* moral consciousness."[117] Although, the presence of "mind" does not explicitly point to intellectual pursuits, it certainly embraces it. Paul is not referring to emotions alone, but to an intelligent approach to life that is renewed through the guidance of the Holy Spirit.[118] In the cultic sense it is a renewal that is achieved and affected by the power and the intervention of God or the Spirit of God. The cultic and sacrificial ritual was common in the ancient world. Hence, there is a wide consensus that Paul takes up the language of sacrifice from the ancient world and redefines the cultic and sacrificial understanding and uses it as a metaphor for a believer's relationship with God.[119]

iii. Living, Holy, and Well-pleasing (Romans 12:1b &2b)

Three characteristics of sacrifice mentioned in the text are living (*zōsan*-ζῶσαν), holy (*hagian*-ἁγίαν), and acceptable (*euareston*-εὐάρεστον-meaning well-pleasing or acceptable) (Rom. 12:1). We see a shift from the temple, shrines, or synagogues to an individual's everyday life activities. There is now a shift from ritual activity to a non-ritual relationship of the individual member within the community of believers as children of God.[120] Hence, the attribute "living" (Rom. 12:1) fits the shift that Paul gives to the ritual language in the understanding of individual beings as a living sacrifice. In Romans 12:1 Paul uses a powerful metaphor to draw his reader's attention. Paul urges his readers to offer their

---

[117] Ladd, *A Theology of the New Testament*, p. 493. The italicized words are mine.

[118] Morris, *The Epistle to the Romans*, p. 435.

[119] See, *BAGD*, p. 628; Dunn, *Romans 9-16*, p. 709. For some Paul follows the tradition in Greek religion, while others explains the language of sacrifice in Romans 12 in line with his Pharisaic background (refer to Jewett and Kotansky, *Romans: A Commentary*, p. 727.

[120] See also, Dunn, *Romans 9-16*, p. 716.

bodies as a living sacrifice. The term living sacrifice stands in contrast to the Jewish cultic setting where blood is spilled. It implies a bloodless sacrifice.[121] Some interpreters appeal to Philo, who spiritualizes the concept of the cult and argue that the intention of Paul in removing sacrifice from the context of the temple was to substitute it with a compliant service in the sacrilegious world.[122] However, when we look into the life and mission of Paul, before his Damascus experience, we are introduced to Saul from a strict Pharisaic Jewish background for whom the temple was very important and he learned the law at the feet of Gamaliel (Acts. 22:3), a well-known and accepted Pharisaic Rabbi during Paul's time. Thus, even after his call to be an apostle of Christ on the road to Damascus, Paul takes pride in his Jewish heritage. He identifies his ethnic root by referring to his heritage as one born of Hebrews and of the Benjamin tribe and circumcised on the eight-day (Phil. 3:5). Then, the question remains how come Paul in Romans 12 emphasized on replacing the temple sacrifice? To address this question, let me refer to Calvin J. Roetzel's view that the integrating center of Paul's theology was his basis and conviction in the death and the resurrection of Jesus Christ. Roetzel argues that Paul views Christ's death through the lens of sacrifice. For instance the sacrificial language in Romans 3:23-25 refers to redemption through the blood of Christ. Roetzel sums his stand and points that "Rather than speaking of the sacrifice of Christ, in 12:1 Paul appropriates sacrificial imagery to initiate a discussion of believing obedience. Calling on and transposing the cultic language from his Pharisaism into a new key Paul appeals to his readers to make a living sacrifice of their bodies and in the most radical sense to become both patron and victim."[123] Paul's understanding of identity and the definition of the people

---

[121] Robert Jewett mentions the diverse literatures that refer to unbloody sacrifices (*Romans: A Commentary*, p. 729. n. 49).

[122] See, Käsemann, *Commentary on Romans*, p. 327; Cranfield, *A Critical and Exegetical Commentary on the Epistle to the Romans*, 2. p. 604.

[123] Calvin J. Roetzel, "Sacrifice in Romans 12-15," *Word & World,* 6/4 (1986), p. 416.

of God are rooted in his Damascus road experience where he encountered the risen Christ (Acts 9). This encounter with Christ on the way to Damascus also changed Paul's perspective on the gospel about Christ Jesus and his self-appropriation as an apostle of Christ. Alan F. Segal also evaluates Paul's Damascus encounter as a social phenomenon, and refers to the encounter as a calling from the risen Christ that changed his perspectives.[124] Thus, Paul's understanding of sacrifice goes back to the Damascus road encounter with the risen Lord, and therefore, he can boldly exhort the believers in Christ as individual living sacrifices and calls on them to actively participate in extending the kingdom of God.

As in a cultic sacrifice, the sacrificial animal and the priest must be ritually pure and worthy for the temple sacrifice and worship, Paul likewise urges the believers in Christ who are a living sacrifice to be holy and well-pleasing to God (Rom. 12:1). Paul calls this sacrifice a "reasonable service" (Rom. 12:1) of the believers in Christ. The attribute "holy" as a cultic concept is dedicated to God and his service, while of persons it stands for humans consecrated to God.[125] It describes the sacrifice that is not profane but solely set apart for the glory of God, i.e., the believers as a living sacrifice. This prerogative of being set apart for the glory of God is extended to the Gentiles who are also sanctified by the Holy Spirit (Rom. 15:16).

The phrase *euareston tō theō* (εὐάρεστον τῷ θεῷ) meaning pleasing to God also appears in the LXX (Wis. 4:10; 9:10) and it is a koine expression.[126] It is an expression depicting an act

---

[124] Alan F. Segal, *Paul the Convert* (New Haven: Yale University Press, 1990).

[125] As a cultic concept, it is also connected to the city of Jerusalem (2Esdras 21; 1Macc. 2:7; Mt. 4:5; 24:15; 27:53; Acts 6:13; 21:28; Rev. 11:2). Of Persons: E.g., Prophets (Lk. 1:70; Acts 3:21; 2Pet. 3:2); John the Baptist (Mk. 6:20); Apostles (Eph. 3:5); Israel (Is. 62:12); Christians (Rom. 1:7; 1 Pet. 1:16). Walter Bauer, *A Greek-English Lexicon of the New Testament and Other Early Christian Literature*, Trans. by William F. Arndt & F. Wilbur Gingrich (1958; Chicago/London: The University of Chicago Press, 1979), p. 9.

[126] Werner Foerster, "εὐάρεστος, εὐάρεστεω," *TDNT* vol. 1 (Grand Rapids, MI:Wm B. Eerdmans 1985), pp. 456-457.

according to the divine force that refers to a sacrifice that is well-pleasing to God. This expression also appears in other Pauline epistles (cf. Rom. 14:18; Phil. 4:18; Col. 3:20).[127] The believers as a living and holy sacrifices are also expected to be acceptable in the sight of God.

Paul concludes his call to be a living, holy and acceptable sacrifice with a threefold apposition "so that you may prove what is the good, acceptable and perfect will of God" (Rom. 12:2b). Paul incorporates the threefold words- good, acceptable, and perfect from concepts of Greco-Roman and Jewish ethics. However, within the context of Romans 12:1-2 there is a transformative use of the Greco-Roman and Jewish concepts.[128] Here, the threefold words, i.e., good, acceptable, and perfect refers to the deeds and everyday affairs and practices that need to be consistent with the will of God because the believers are expected to be living sacrifices, holy and acceptable (Rom. 12:1). Theodore Zahn also asserts that in 12:2, good, acceptable, perfect, are not three attributes of God, but are guidelines to evaluate the actions and works of believers as consistent or inconsistent with the will of God.[129] It describes the living standards according to the will of God. In the Hebrew wisdom tradition and Rabbinic ethics, Hellenistic Judaism, classical and later Greek philosophy and the Roman value system "good" stands for the highest moral quality.[130] The term *euarestos* (εὐάρεστος) meaning acceptable elicits a widely approved realm of sophistic and public ethics as it appears without attribution to God.[131] This same connotation is also explicit in Romans 12:1. The term *teleios* (τέλειος) meaning perfect and its equivalents depict the highest realm of moral and spiritual insight in Hebrew,

---

[127] See also, Jewett, *Romans*, p. 729.

[128] See also, Jewett, *Romans*, p. 734.

[129] Theodore Zahn, *Der Brief des Paulus an die Römer*. Kommentar zum Neuen Testament 6 (Leipzig: Deichert, 1910), pp. 539-540.

[130] Walter Grundmann, "ἀγαθὸς," *TDNT*, vol. 1 (1964), pp. 10-15.

[131] Jewett, *Romans*, pp. 734-735. It also appears in the context of slavery where the slaves satisfy the masters through their deeds and conduct (Tit. 2:9).

Greek, and Latin thought.[132] The threefold category implies that every ethical category calls for transformation and the basis for the transformation are the "mercies of God" and the "renewal of the mind" which are revealed in Christ.[133] Thus, the renewal of the mind enables the believers to live a transformed life following the will of God that demands standard human values of goodness, well-pleasing, and perfect. Abiding by such standard guidelines in a believer's life guide him/her to a renewed relationship with God. Consequently, Paul exhorts the believers not to put on the mindset that is practiced by the Roman society, but to focus on the "mercies of God."

Thus, in the context of a believer's personal life as a follower of Christ Paul applies the cultic language of living, holy and acceptable. As indicated, they depict an expression of a believer's faith, being, and action by the will of God. For Paul being a living offering, holy and well-pleasing transforms a believer's life through the renewing of the mind. Such a transformed life helps in relating and connecting to God through Christ at a personal level. Consequently, staying righteous before God also contributes to a believer's relationship within members of the believing community to which we now turn.

The Community Sphere: Christ Believing Community (Romans 12:3-13)

The Christ believing community is addressed in Romans 12:3-13. In these verses Paul describes the corporate identity of the Christ believing community. Paul's exhortation in Romans 12:3 touches the question of social hierarchy and the privileged prevalent in Roman society.

i. High Thoughts versus Sober-Minded (Romans 12:3)

A syntactical construction in Romans 12:3 is the wordplay on the Greek verb *phronein* (φρονεῖν), which is translated as "to think."

---

[132] Gerhard Delling, "τέλειος," *TDNT* vol. 8 (1972), pp. 67-72.

[133] Jewett, *Romans*, pp. 735. Other Pauline texts are 1 Cor. 1:28; 13:10; 14:20.

Two other Greek verbs in Romans 12:3 that are connected to *phronein* (φρονεῖν) are the modifiers *huperphronein* (ὑπερφρονεῖν) meaning to have high thoughts and *sōphronein* (σωφρονεῖν) meaning to be sober-minded. Paul begins with *phronein* (φρονεῖν) and the modifier *huperphronein* (ὑπερφρονεῖν) and then attaches the negative mē (μὴ) exhorting his readers "not to have high thoughts" or "not to think highly." This is followed by *phronein* (φρονεῖν) and the modifier *huperphronein* (ὑπερφρονεῖν) in the articular infinitive construction *alla phronein eis to sōphronein* (ἀλλὰ φρονεῖν εἰς τὸ σωφρονεῖν), which means "but to think soberly." The construction of beginning with a negative imperative followed by articular infinitive construction in the use of the word "to think" highlights the approach and quality in which the believers in Christ are expected to think.[134] James Dunn explores further by observing this Greek construction within the Hellenistic philosophy and claims that Paul's recipients' could be familiar with such construction because the root word was generally used in "popular Hellenistic philosophy denoting modesty and restraint" and was considered as a fundamental virtue.[135] Paul uses the same verb with a similar construction in his other Epistles as in 2Corinthians 5:13, which reads, "for whether we are mad, *it is* to God; or we are sober-minded, *it is* for you." As seen in the previous chapter, in the Roman society those with superior social status and legal privileges took pride in their status and maintained their superior social status in all levels of social and political life. As a counter-teaching to the social superiors and inferiors in the Roman social hierarchy, Paul calls the believers in Christ in Rome "not to think more highly than what is necessary to think" (Rom. 12:3). It is a call to think soberly and to exercise their role and responsibility according to the measure of faith that God has assigned. The way one thinks or regards oneself should not be on the basis of social hierarchy and class distinctions as it is practiced in the Roman social order and structure, but by the will of God.

---

[134] Along this line of interpretation is also Moo, *The Epistle to the Romans*, p. 760.

[135] Dunn, *Romans 9-16*, p. 721.

The Greeks incorporated principles of their culture known as *arête, which are moral virtues,* connected to the notion of excellent living. Among the virtues (*arête*) *sophrosyne*, which means sober-minded, was difficult to assimilate to the Roman virtues, as it was more common in the Greek society than the Roman society. It expresses self-knowledge and self-control, which was demanded by the citizens in the cities. It was emphasized in order to combat individualism and self-assertion. Thus, *sophrosyne*, which was common during the Hellenistic Period as an individual exercise of self-control, was incorporated into the Christian faith. Self-control also applied to food and drink and to all areas of human life.[136] In the gospels the concept of virtue in line with the classical Greek understanding is found in the beatitudes, and the life of Christ, especially his humility. There are also instances in the gospels (Mk. 5:15; Lk. 8:35) of the use of *sophronounto* within the context of being clothed in a tight mind after the exorcism. *Sophrosyne* in opposition to the tyranny of the appetites indicates self-control and we find it in the context of clothing (1Tim. 2:9) and the office of a church leader (1Tim. 3:2; Titus 1:8). In Paul's epistles *sophrosyne* appears in exhortations on ethics and morality. We find three aspects of *sophrosyne* in Paul's epistles and Acts, i.e., in opposition to madness, to pride, and the tyranny of the appetites. *Sophrosyne* as in opposition to the madness is found in Acts 26:25 where Paul replies, "I am not mad, most excellent Festus, but I speak forth words of truth and *sophrosyne*." *Sophrosyne* in opposition to pride is found in Romans 12:3 recalling the Hellenistic commonplaces of "self-knowledge and thinking mortal thoughts." Paul urges the believers not to think too highly of themselves, but to practice modest thoughts.[137]

Having high thoughts was a virtue practiced by those in power. The Greek word *hubris* generally translated as arrogance

---

[136] Helen North, *Sophrosyne: Self-Knowledge and Self-Restraint in Greek Literature*, Cornell Studies in Classical Philology, vol. XXXV (New York: Cornell University Press, 1966), pp. 228 & 258.

[137] For discussions on *sophrosyne* in this paragraph refer to North, *Sophrosyne* refer to North, *Sophrosyne*, pp. 316-317.

or extreme or foolish pride has social effects and Paul brings this concept in his other epistles as well (1 Cor. 1-3; 2 Cor. 10-13). Throughout the classical Greek and Hellenistic philosophy and literature, *hubris* is connected to arrogance and insolence that comes from the ignorance of self-knowing. It is a social concept where a breach of a person's assigned status and undue pride in strength and wealth can lead to dishonor and shame.[138] In Greek philosophy *hubris* is generally treated as a non-religious concept that takes place in a moral and social context.

In Romans 12:3 Paul's usage of the virtue *sophronein* (σωφρονεῖν) meaning sober-minded has classical sense and it is close to political usage. Halvor Moxnes suggest that Paul appears comfortable with the Hellenistic use of *sophrosyne* in Romans 12. As such, his exhortation to the believers not to think highly of oneself is directed to "a total system of relations between individuals of unequal status."[139] In Romans 12:3 it supports the communal meaning, especially when used in connection with the body metaphor in Romans 12:4-5.[140] The different parts of the body and its contribution through diverse charismatic gifts enforce the relations expected in a community. In Romans 12:3 *sophronein* (σωφρονεῖν), which means sober-minded, is used in contrast to *huperphronein* (ὑπερφρονεῖν), which means to have high thoughts or to think highly of oneself. Paul urges believers in Christ to be sober-minded and refrain from thinking highly of oneself. This clearly suggests a relational motif in accepting and respecting one another.

ii. Metaphor of a Body (Romans 12:4-8)

The teaching against social hierarchy and status is developed further with the use of the analogy of the human body in Romans

---

[138] Peter Marshall, *Enmity in Corinth: Social Conversations in Paul's relation with the Corinthians* (Tübingen: Mohr Siebeck, 1987), pp. 193-194.

[139] Moxnes, "The Quest for Honor and the Unity…," p. 222.

[140] Halvor Moxnes, "The Quest for Honor and the Unity of the community in Romans 12 and in the Orations of Dio Chrysostom," *Paul in his Hellenistic Context*, Ed. Troels Engberg-Pedersen (Edinburgh: T&T Clark, 1994), p. 221.

12:4-5. The body metaphor in the context of the community of believers in Christ is elaborated in 1 Corinthians 12:12-26. In Romans, we find the abbreviated form of the body metaphor. It is accepted that the body metaphor in 1 Corinthinas is closer to the Roman story of the strife between senators and plebeians in Rome. This story is ascribed to Menenius Agrippa. The plebeians threatened with mutiny and the senators realized that harmony among the citizens was threatened, therefore Menenius Agrippa was sent to the plebeians. In order to make peace Agrippa told a fable using a body. He indicated to the threatening effects when conflicts arise between the various members of the body. The fable of the body was used in order to indicate that strife was dangerous and therefore it was important to restore harmony. In 1 Corinthians the body imagery is applied in the context of conflict arising because of diverse charismatic gifts. However, in Romans 12 Paul uses it as a basis for unity by only alluding to the conflict and not confronting it.[141] Paul's concern is to bring Jewish believers in Christ and the Gentile believers together by accepting and building up one another. Boasting is an attitude of the Jews, especially based on their knowledge and their long faith tradition (Rom. 2:17). Therefore, he reminds the Roman believers that they have all sinned and fall short of the glory of God.

The metaphor of a body as a single entity, yet, made up of diverse parts that are interdependent is a familiar image, which Paul uses in Romans and in 1 Corinthians 12. In Romans 12:6-8 the body analogy is elaborated within the context of the community of believers in Christ. The community of believers in Christ is interdependent as a body, where the individual members bring their gifts and contribute to the building and the growth of the community. Paul reminds the Roman believers that their gifts as individuals are not measured according to the social hierarchy and status, but it is measured through faith and their gifts should be utilized for building and transforming the community. Although, in the Roman society, social status defined one's place in the society, Paul moves beyond social hierarchies and reminds the

[141] Moxnes, "The Quest for Honor and the Unity...," p. 224.

believers of their diverse roles in relating to other members within the believers' community, not in relation to social status and privileges, but in the believers' allegiance to God.

iii. The Motif of Love, Honor, and Hospitality (Romans 12:9-13)

In contrast to the Roman practice of conflict and enmity, Paul exhorts the Roman believers in Christ on handling conflicts and adversaries in Romans 12:9-13. He calls for love, to honor one another, and to practice hospitality. Paul addresses the believers in Christ in Rome to honor one another. The Greek word *proēgoumenoi* (προηγούμενοι) means, "take the lead" or "precede." So it means to go before others in order to show the way. Still, occasionally it is also translated in some versions like Old Latin, Vulgate, Syriac, and Armenian as "outdo." In reference to honor the versions translate the Greek phrase *tē timē allēlous proēgoumenoi* (τῇ τιμῇ ἀλλήλους προηγούμενοι 12:10) meaning outdo one another in showing respect.[142] Thus, Paul in Romans 12:10 is urging the believers in Christ to "take the lead" in honoring one another at all times without expecting anything in return. In Roman society honor was a response to an act of beneficence. Paul reverses the honor system of the Roman society by urging the believers in Christ to show honor rather than to expect honor from others[143] and departs from the competitive spirit attached to the honor system.[144] Within the community of believers in Christ, Halvor Moxnes points out that God becomes the significant other and only God can praise and pass judgment upon an individual member.[145] Similarly, John Barclay asserts that "honour does not

---

[142] Bauer, *A Greek-English Lexicon of the New Testament*, p. 706. For outdo also refer to Halvor Moxnes, "Honor and Righteousness in Rome," *JSNT* 32 (1988), p. 71.

[143] So also, Oakes, *Reading Romans in Pompeii*, 110; Elliott, "Political Paul and the Social Context of Romans 12-13," p. 8.

[144] Halvor Moxnes, "Honor and Righteousness in Rome," *JSNT* 32 (1988), p. 75.

[145] Shohe, *Acceptance Motif in Paul: Revisiting Romans 15:7-13.*

have to be sought: all the honour that counts has already been given, or will be given, by God."[146]

Paul exhorts the Roman believers to honor one another in love. He employs the Greek word *Philadelphia* (φιλαδελφία) referring to sisterly/brotherly love,[147] a love given without expecting anything in return. Paul calls the believers to love a brother and sister in faith as members of the family of God. In this imperative to the believing community "to take the lead" to honor one another, Paul moves beyond the honor system in the Greco-Roman society and redirects honor to the level of taking initiative in love regardless of status. The basis for growing together as a believing community is love. With the use of an attribute of love, i.e., *anupokritos* (ἀνυπόκριτος) (Rom. 12:10) meaning genuine, un-assumed, Paul calls for sincere love, a love without hypocrisy (cf. 2 Cor. 6:6; Rom. 13:10; Mt. 24:12). Thus, the Greek word used for love is an intimate and close bond love, i.e., sibling love. It is not an outward expression of care and concern for the other, but it is a love that accepts and cares regardless of ethnic and social differences.

Paul ends his ethical teaching within the community of the believers in Christ with the notion of hospitality. Two Greek words in the New Testament are used for hospitality. One is *philoxenia*[148] *means "lover of a stranger." The Greek word philo* is an expression of love and *xenos* means "stranger" or "someone we have no knowledge of."[149] Thus I would translate it as "love of a stranger." The other Greek word in the New Testament for hospitality is *xenodocheo* (in 1Tim. 5:10). As mentioned *xenos* means stranger and *dechomai* means "receive," "accept," "take with hand" or

---

[146] Barclay, *Paul and the Gift*, p. 510.

[147] Spencer Elliott refers to it as sibling-love ("Political Paul and the Social Context of Romans 12-13," p. 9). Some refer to "brotherly love" (Charles Lee Irons, *A Syntax Guide for Readers of the Greek New Testament* (Grand Rapids, MI: Kregel), p. 360.

[148] This word is used in Romans 12:13; 1Timothy 3:2; Titus 1:8; Hebrews 13:2; 1Peter 4:9.

[149] "Prevenient Grace:" The Theological term for Hospitality. *Dotheword.org.*

"embrace."[150] In Romans 12:13 Paul calls the believers to "pursue hospitality" by using the Greek words *philoxinian diōkontes*.[151] As seen from the two Greek words used for hospitality in the New Testament, hospitality is not only being nice to people we know, but it also means making space for strangers in our lives, our communities, and our churches. Hospitality is taking by the hand and embracing the "other" into our community.

Many exegetes acknowledge that based on the context *philoxinian* should be translated as hospitality in Romans 12:13.[152] Robert Jewett assumes that there is no further elaboration on "hospitality to strangers" because the ethic of love is elaborated in Romans 12. So, for Jewett hospitality is already encompassed in Paul's description of love ethic.[153] In line with Jewett I would interpret Paul's call to pursue hospitality in Romans 12:13 within the context of love ethic as a call to love strangers like they were siblings in a family. The ethic of hospitality was widely practiced in ancient society, which includes the Greco-Roman and Jewish society. In ancient society the temples and altars were places of asylum. In Maccabees 6:2 Zeus is considered a protector of the rights of hospitality. Similarly, in Judaism there are references to Israel's experience as "strangers in Egypt" (Lev. 19:34; Deu. 10:19). Abraham is also considered a model of hospitality in his act of welcoming the three heavenly visitors in Genesis 18.[154] Therefore, hospitality would have been an expected obligation. Also the context of the lapse of the Claudian Edict after the death of Claudius and the return of the Jews and believers in Christ to Rome demanded hospitality in order to avoid future conflicts and

---

150 "Prevenient Grace:" The Theological term for Hospitality. *Dotheword.org.*

151 James Dunn translates the Greek words as "aspire to hospitality" (Dunn, *Romans 9-16*, p. 743).

152 Dunn, *Romans 9-16*, 743; Jewett, *Romans*, 765; Fitzmyer, *Romans*, p. 655.

153 Jewett, *Romans*, p. 765.

154 Dunn, *Romans 9-16*, p. 743.

hostilities.[155] The city of Rome was a metropolitan city where traders and travelers and those seeking jobs and a better life would come into the city. Hence, being a city where outsiders and visitors flocked into, the obligation of being hospitable would be important. As such, Paul rounds off his exhortation in Romans 12:1-13 with a call to sincere love and the practice of hospitality.

Thus, we see that in Romans 12:3-13 Paul is exhorting the community of the believers in Christ. In the midst of the wider Roman society where status, wealth, birth and positions decided one's place in the society, Paul calls on the community of the believers in Christ by using the metaphor of a body towards sober-thinking and functioning of their gifts and responsibilities by practicing love, honor, and hospitality towards one another. In such thinking and practice relationships can grow and it can be strengthened.

The Social and Civil Sphere: Larger Society within the Imperial Milieu

The social and civil sphere is indicated in Romans 12:14-21 and 13:1-10. The believers in Christ cannot live in isolation from the wider world but require the wider social environment.

i. Romans 12:14-21 and the Larger Society

In Romans 12:14-21 Paul is exhorting the believers in Christ in relating and living side by side with individuals and groups outside the Christian faith community. This would have been important because Christian faith was not the faith of the Roman Empire, but it was also among the many faith groups that existed in the Roman Empire. Consequently, it would have been important for Paul to emphasize the external dimension of the context for peaceful co-existence.

Two different views are proposed by interpreters regarding the setting of Romans 12:14-21. One view is that Romans 12:14-

---

[155] For elaborate reading on the Claudian Edict and the context of Romans refer to my monograph, *Acceptance Motif in Paul: Revisiting Romans 15:7-13*. Also Jewett, *Romans*, p. 765.

21 is connected to Romans 12:1-13. Those who take this view argue for an ecclesial focus and not the wider social context. They identify the "persecutors" and "enemies" as members within the community of the believers in Christ. For them, living in harmony and associating with the lowly (Rom. 12:16) reflects a community relation and not an outside force. They are also of the opinion that Paul in Romans 12:14-21 is in line with the Jewish traditions in bringing these elements together to instruct and respond to those suffering in the hands of the fellow believers.[156] The other and the more widely accepted hypothesis argues that Romans 12:1-13 is addressed to the community of the believers in Christ, while Romans 12: 14-21 is addressed to the outsiders. They affirm their view by pointing to the shift from internal to external setting in Romans 12:14 where Paul refers to non-believing persecutors.[157] Some interpreters have noted the interruption of thought and a shift from verse 13 to verse 14. For example, Charles Talbert takes Romans 12: 14, 15, 16c, 17b, 19b, and 20 as redactional that was added to "a traditional unit of ethical instructions, originating probably in Semitic Christianity."[158] Along this line, Ernst Käsemann also points out that there is no consistent flow of thought because this section is taken from Jewish sapiential sayings where different elements are brought together.[159]

---

[156] D. A. Black, "The Pauline Love Command Structure, Style and Ethics in Romans 12:9-21," *Filologia Neotestamentaria*, 2 (1989): pp. 9-10; K. Yinger, "Romans 12:14-21 and Nonretaliation in Second Temple Judaism: Addressing Persecution within the Community," (January 1998). *Faculty Publications-George Fox Evangelical Seminary*. Paper 62. https://digitalcommons.georgefox.edu/gfes/62 (accessed on March 27, 2020). (Note: since this is an HTML document, there are no page numbers).

[157] Cranfield, *A Critical and Exegetical Commentary on the Epistle to the Romans*, 2. pp. 629-630; 640-641; Dunn, *Romans 9-16*, pp. 737-739; J. A. Ziesler, *Paul's Letter to the Romans* (TPI New Testament Commentaries; London: SCM, 1989), p. 303.

[158] Charles Talbert, "Traditions and Redactions in Romans XII. 9-21," *New Testament Studies*, 16 (1969-1970), p. 91.

[159] Käsemann, *Commentary on Romans*, pp. 345-347.

However, to refer to Romans 12 as a loosely organized collection cannot be sustained by the text. A close reading of the text, i.e., Romans 12-13 shows Paul's exhortation to the believers in Christ regarding their roles and identity within the ecclesial context and also outside the ecclesial community. This is because the ecclesial community is not removed from the world to the heavenly realm, but it continues to exist and participate in the everyday life and affairs of the world. This study is in line with the hypothesis that in Romans 12:14-21 Paul's exhortation incorporates the external dimensions of context from verse 14 onwards. In the text, we find general references concerning those that persecute, or a plea to be part of those who are rejoicing as well as those that are weeping. There is also an appeal to repay no one with evil and instead to provide good things before all men and seek peace with all men (Rom.12:17-18). The reference to *pantōn anthrōpōn* (πάντων ἀνθρώπων) meaning all men appears in Romans 12:17-18. Some interpreters use the Greek words *anthrōpos* and *anēr* to make an argument for an inclusive and specific person. Those who support this argument affirm that *anthrōpos* cannot mean "man" on a limited sense of "male human being," but it has an inclusive understanding of "human being." In contrast the Greek word *anēr* is gender-specific and refers to a "male human being."[160] However, the Greek semantics does not support it, and also the Greek word *anēr* emphasizes the masculinity of the person referred or based on the context it is also translated as husband and *anthrōpos* is used for a male human being. The Greek word *anthrōpos* (ἀνθρώπος) in its singular form is used for a particular person or individual refers specifically to man/male. Yet, in its plural form the Greek word *anthrōpos* does not refer to "man" in its limited sense, but it is used in a gender-inclusive sense, provided that it is permitted by the context of the text. Still, the absence of any contextual indications may mean

[160] This view is supported by Donald A. Carson, *The Inclusive Language Debate: A Plea for Realism* (Grand Rapids: Baker, 1998), pp. 126-127.

otherwise.[161] In Romans 12:17-18 the plural *anthrōpōn* can be translated as human beings because the context of the text also permits it. Paul reminds the believers in Christ of their roles and responsibilities in extending their good works to all human beings. This is supported by the use of *pantōn* with *anthrōpōn* indicating a wider connotation of all human beings and not all believers. Thus, we can conclude that from Romans 12:14 onwards, external aspects outside the community of the believers in Christ are incorporated.

ii. Ethical Commands in Relating to the Larger Society

In Romans 12:14-21 Paul addresses the Roman believers of their roles in relating to the communities outside the Christian faith communities. Here, Paul brings a few ethical commands that emphasize on creating a peaceful and caring environment. He especially emphasizes on the task and the response of the believers in Christ in relating to individuals and groups outside the Christ believing community.

Interpreters of Romans have different views in understanding "those that persecute" in Romans 12:14. Gordon Zerbe asserts that the verb *diōkein* (διωκειν) meaning to persecute in other Pauline epistles and New Testament books refer "to hostility from outsiders, never from insiders."[162] However, Kent Yinger refers to this hypothesis as oversimplifying the actual situation. Yinger does a thorough analysis and presents a convincing hypothesis. He identifies references from the New Testament where *diōkein* (διωκειν) also refers to internal persecution or persecution within the community and supports his stand with scriptural references. The use of *diōkein* (διωκειν) as an intra

---

[161] For details on the linguistic discussion, see Vern S. Poythress, "Male Meaning in Generic Masculines in Koine Greek," *Westminster Theological Journal*, 66/2 (2004): pp. 325-326; Michael D. Marlowe, "The Ambiguity of Anthropos," (2003). http://www.bible-researcher.com/anthropos.html (accessed on May 14, 2020).

[162] Zerbe, *Non-Retaliation in Early Jewish and New Testament Texts* p. 227. A. Oepke, "διωκω," *TDNT* 2, pp. 229-230.

Jewish opponent (Mt. 5:12; 23: 34; Lk. 11:49) and the persecution of the disciples of Jesus (whom he regards as Jews) by other Jews (Mt. 5:10-12; 10:16-23; Lk. 21:12-19). Therefore, Yinger argues that even in Pauline epistles, Paul can use *diōkein* (διωκειν) in referring to "Jewish (-Christian) opponents of his gospel."[163] Yet, the problem with Yinger's argument lies in a very general conclusion for all the epistles of Paul. There is a need to investigate Paul's letters within its diverse context and circumstances. Therefore, in generalizing the use of *diōkein* (διωκειν) in the Pauline epistles we sideline and overlook the context. In Romans 12-13:10 Paul's exhortation is addressed to the believers in Christ in relating to different people, groups, and situations. As discussed above in Romans 12:3-13 Paul is addressing the community of believers in relating to one another. He uses the body metaphor by identifying gifts within an ecclesial context. Then, from Romans 12:14-21 Paul uses words and phrases that have broader implications (discussed above under the section *Romans 12:14-21 and the Broader Society*). Yinger also overlooks the context of Paul's address in Romans 13, which is referring to those outside the believing community. The use of adjectival participle *tous diökontas* (τοὺς διώκοντας) (Rom. 12:14) refers to the agent of persecution, that is, those who are persecuting another. Here, Paul is asking the believer in Christ to bless the persecutors and not to curse them (Rom. 12:14).

From Romans 12:17-21 we find similarity in form and the style of ethical commands in the exhortation in Romans 12 and the teachings of Jesus' Sermon on the Mount in Matthew 5. We. As in the Sermon on the Mount, Paul's ethical command also begins negatively and this is followed by a positive command.[164]

---

[163] Yinger, "Romans 12:14-21 and Nonretaliation in Second Temple Judaism."

[164] Eric K. C. Wong, "The De-radicalization of Jesus' Ethical Sayings in Romans," in *Novum Testamentum*, 43/3 (2001): pp. 245-251; Paul W. Meyer, "Romans" in *Harper Collins Biblical Commentary*, ed. James L. Mays (San Francisco, CA: Harper San Francisco, 2000), p. 1068; W. Wink, *Engaging the Powers: Discernment and Resistance in a World of Domination* (Minneapolis, MN: Fortress Press, 1992), pp. 185-186.

In Romans 12:17-21 we find pairs like recompense no one for evil, but live peaceably with all (vv. 17-18); avenge no one, but practice hospitality towards enemies (vv. 19-20); be not overcome of evil, but overcome evil with good (v. 21).[165] These pairs begin with a prohibition by Paul exhorting the believers in Christ to abstain from a negative action, which is then followed by a positive action that can help in connecting positively with others and building transformative relations.

Paul calls the believers in Christ to set an exemplary lifestyle based on harmony and growing together by uplifting one another in Romans 12:14-21. Bruce Winter provides an interpretation of Romans 12:14-21 as a counter-cultural response to strife and jealousy in the relationships among members within the Roman society. For Winter the class distinctions both in public and private entertainment and the enmity relationships in Roman law were established Roman behaviors and practices. Against such behaviors and practices Paul in Romans 12 brings up the will of God for his people and calls the believers to the will of God.[166]

The believers in Christ are encouraged to bless even those that persecute them (Rom. 12:14) and to live peaceably with all by extending the good works and hospitality to those outside the boundary of family and community (Rom. 12:17-21). Gordon Zerbe discusses this particular text in the context of Paul's non-violent gospel and makes a noteworthy observation that the non-violent Jesus as presented in the saying of Jesus in Luke 6:27-28 and Matthew 5:44 is reflected in Paul's letters, especially in Romans 12:14. The sayings of Jesus could have existed in different forms, which Paul also had access to.[167] The teaching on the right living with the outside world is broadened in Romans 13:8-10 through the ethic of love. This ethic becomes a basis for a relationship with those outside the Christian faith

---

[165] See also, Moo, *The Epistle to the Romans*, p. 785.

[166] Winter, "Roman Law and Society in Romans 12-15," pp. 80-81.

[167] Gordon Zerbe, *Non-Retaliation in Early Jewish and New Testament Texts: Ethical Themes in Social Contexts* (Bloomsbury: T&T Clark, 1993), 58-63.

communities. Amid the threats or hostility from the outside forces because of their faith in Christ, the believers in Christ are encouraged to be at peace with all people. The principles of building healthy communities are thus extended to the wider social context. In particular Paul exhorts the believers in Christ in their attitude and behavior towards the superior authorities within the Roman Empire.

iii. Commands in Relating to Superior Authorities

Paul brings his exhortation in relating to the privileged and the superior authorities in Romans 13:1-7. Two areas in which the role of the superior authorities is mentioned in Romans 13:1-4: first, they are ordained by God to carry their responsibilities in keeping law and order; second, they have the obligation to praise those who carry out good works. In Roman society the superior authorities were to praise or honor its members for any form of civil service to the city, just as honoring and praising those in authority for their civil and public contribution was common in the Roman and Greek society. Paul was likely aware of influential individuals within the Roman believing communities who could undertake some benefactions (as some names imply in Rom. 16). Hence, Paul calls the believers in Christ to do good so that they may receive praise from the superior authority (13:3).[168] Paul further outlines the requirements of the believers in Christ towards the superior authorities in Romans 13:5-7. In Romans 13:5-6 the believers in Christ are to be subject to the superior authorities since they are ambassadors of God to rule and govern the people justly.

Paul sums up the section in Romans 13:7 by laying before his readers a few obligations. The obligations laid before the believers are connected to tribute (φόρον-*phoron*), taxes (τέλος-*telos*), fear (φόβον-*phobon*), and honor (τιμὴν-*timēn*). Bruce Winter refers to these obligations as 'tangible' and 'intangible' obligations. For Winter, tribute (φόρον-*phoron*), and taxes (τέλος-

[168] For this interpretation see Winter, "Roman Law and Society in Romans 12-15," 81-83.

telos) stands for 'tangible' obligations and fear (φόβον-*phobon*), and honor (τιμὴν-*timēn*) for 'intangible' obligations.[169] Taxes and tribute are two different forms of state revenue. Tribute was levied on people and land and it was required for everyone both Roman citizens and non-Roman citizens living in the empire to pay tributes.[170] Paul exhorts to pay tribute to those who are entitled to get tribute. Likewise, in the Gospel according to Luke there are also references to paying tribute to Caesar (Lk. 20:22; 23:2). Taxes refer to indirect tax or customs duties.[171] Taxes were levied on income, services, and goods that were sold in markets controlled by the Roman authorities in Rome and the entire Roman Empire. Taxes were important sources of revenue within the Roman Empire.[172] Paul calls on the believers in Christ to pay taxes that are due to the Roman Empire because believers in Christ were also part of the larger social set up in the Roman Empire. Fear (φόβον-*phobon*) refers to fear or terror (1Pet. 3:14). It can be the fear of the Lord as in 2 Corinthians 5:11 or can refer to arousing fear and terror in a person as in Romans 13:3. It is also translated as reverence and respect when it refers to Christ (Phil 2:12). If it is directed towards a person then respect is used, as respect that is due to officials (Romans 13:7a), or slave to master (1Pet. 2:18; 3:2; Eph. 6:5)[173] Thus, Paul is calling for giving due respect to the superior authorities as they are also appointed to oversee the well-being of the city, state and to exercise order. The Greek word *timē* (τιμὴ) in the context of selling and buying means price or value (Mt. 27:9; Acts 4:34; 19:19). It can also mean showing of honor or reverence or respect as an action (Rom. 12:10; 1Tim. 6:1) or honor as a possession (cf. 1Pet. 2:7; 1Cor 12:24; Rev. 4:9). In

---

[169] Winter, "Roman Law and Society in Romans 12-15," 83.

[170] Winter, "Roman Law and Society in Romans 12-15," 83-84.

[171] Other references are 1Macc. 10:31; 11:35; Josephus, Ant. 12.141. See Bauer, *A Greek-English Lexicon*, 811-812.

[172] L. de. Ligt, *Fairs and Markets in the Roman Empire: Economic and Social aspects of Periodic Trade in a Pre-industrial Society* (Amsterdam: J. C. Gieben, 1993), 169.

[173] Bauer, *A Greek-English Lexicon of the New Testament*, 863-864.

Romans 13:7 it is brought out in Paul's teachings to the members of the Christian faith towards superior authorities and so it can refer to the respect that one enjoys because of one's position in the society.[174]

Robert Jewett asserts that in Romans 8:38 the principalities and powers are identified as opponents, but in Romans 13:1-7 Paul's exhortation on being subject to authorities probably reflects a time when believers in Christ are already at peace with the world.[175] Ernst Käsemann claims that the notion of authorities as God's servant is "obviously exaggerated if not wholly incredible." Thus, for Käsemann it is a traditional material that Paul appealed to.[176]A few interpreters refer to Romans 13:1-7 as an interpolation because in Romans 12 Paul admonishes believers in Christ not to think too highly of oneself. This indicates that he was opposing the honor system in Roman culture. However, in Romans 13:1-7 Paul's emphasis is on being subjects to authorities and also incorporates the language of fear towards the authorities.[177] It is unlikely that Romans 13:1-7 is an interpolation or that Paul inserts it blindly into this section of Romans, especially when read within the historical context of Romans, i.e., the Claudian Edict of 49 CE (as discussed in Chapter Two). No doubt, in these verses Paul makes an abrupt transition, as we do not find conjunction or a particle that joins these verses with the preceding pericope. However, the subject matter Paul takes up is in line with the teachings in Romans 12-15 and it presents Paul's concern concerning the boundaries of the Christian faith community with the outside world, particularly to the political authorities with the emperor as the head.

---

[174] Bauer, *A Greek-English Lexicon*, 817-818.

[175] Jewett, *Romans*, 783.

[176] Käsemann, *Commentary on Romans*, 357-359; Ernst Käsemann, "Principles in the Interpretation of Romans 13," *New Testament Questions of Today*, Trans. W. J. Montague (Philadelphia: Fortress Press, 1969), 200.

[177] James Kallas, "Romans XIII:1-7: An Interpolation," *NTS*, 11 (1964-65), 365-374; Winsome Munro, *Authority in Paul and Peter*, SNTS MonographSer 45 (Cambridge: Cambridge University Press, 1983), 79.

Romans 13:1-7 is interpreted as an admonition of Paul to the Roman believers in Christ to restrain from creating unrest that would threaten the already hostile relationship between the Roman believers and the Jewish population.[178] The social context in which Paul brings his teachings in Romans 13:1-7 is likely in connection to the tax protest of AD 58.[179] During the early years of the emperorship of Claudius, he canceled taxes that were imposed by his predecessors like the granting to procurators of the right to levy taxes. However, after the death of Claudius, under the emperorship of Nero, he increased the level of taxes and introduced new taxes.[180] His teachings on the obligations fitting to the superior authorities reflect the time of the returning Jews and Jewish believers in Christ who were expelled from Rome during the time of Emperor Claudius in AD 49 (as discussed in chapter two).[181] Paul did not want the believers in Christ to attract the attention of the Roman authorities by denying the obligations that were due to the Roman authorities in the form of tax, honor, tribute, and fear. The Jews because of their ancestral religion had special privileges to practice their ancestral customs, which included temple tax to be sent to Jerusalem. Yet, Paul's redefinition of the people of God could no longer claim political privileges.[182] Before the Claudian expulsion the Roman authority did not differentiate between Jews and believers in Christ as they worshiped in the Synagogue. Therefore, the believers in Christ also enjoyed the privileges given to the Jews because of their long faith tradition.

---

[178] Neil Elliott, "Romans 13:1–7 in the Context of Imperial Propaganda," in R. A. Horsley, ed., *Paul and Empire: Religion and Power in Roman Imperial Society*, p. 196; see also Elliott, *Liberating Paul*, 221–26. Also, Klaus Wengst, *Pax Romana and the Peace of Jesus Christ*, Trans. John Bowden (SCM Press, 1987), 102-104.

[179] Tacitus, *Annals* 13.50 [http://penelope.uchicago.edu] (accessed on August, 2019).

Seutonius, *Nero* 44:1-2 [http://penelope.uchicago.edu] (accessed on August, 2019).

[180] Seutonius, *Nero* 44.

[181] Shohe, *Acceptance Motif in Paul: Revisiting Romans 15:7-13*.

[182] Dunn discusses it in *Romans 9-16*, 769.

However, after the expulsion it would have been evident to the Roman authorities that Jewish tradition and Christian faith are different. This also meant the believers in Christ could no longer claim the privileges that the Jews had access to. Thus, it is likely that Paul is exhorting the Christian faith communities to be careful and responsible as the situation in Rome was still sensitive and volatile. Paul did not want the believers in Christ to create another havoc and bring about divisions among themselves. He wanted them to lead a peaceful life and therefore he directs them to live and act by the political demands of the Roman society and the imperial order.[183] These demands include being subject to the superior authority and paying of taxes. It is therefore likely that Paul brings his teachings on submitting to the official power and authority. Governing authority is supposed to exist for good governance and also for the smooth functioning of the society, although there are also times when the powers are misused. Paul affirms that the political authority comes from God and so any resistance to this God-given responsibility is also a resistance to the command of God.

Romans 12-13 and the Larger Roman Society

From the above study of the text we can conclude that in Romans 12 Paul envisages a community where members do not seek personal and individual honor. Paul's exhortation in Romans 12:3-13 is directed to relations within the community of believers. Paul wanted to check the control of ambitious living, and thoughts among the believers in Christ. Paul begins in Romans 12:3 against being over self-ambitious, self-exaltation, and self-centered. Instead, Paul calls for giving honor to one another and associating with the lowly. In inculcating such an attitude Paul believes that divisions within the community of believers can be overcome. Paul's exhortation is directed against arrogant attitude

---

[183] See also Elliott, *The Arrogance of the Nations*, 154. James Dunn also refers to the Claudian Edict as the background as already discussed in chapter two.

and behavior and against honor and status consciousness in a society (Rom. 12:3, 9-10, 16).

Paul in Romans 12 is concerned with the practices relating to the ethos of the city that concerns honor-shame. Paul here indirectly attacks the "honor culture" that was widely prevalent in the Greco-Roman society. Halvor Moxnes discusses the honor and status in Romans 12 within the Hellenistic context. He asserts that the Hellenistic concepts and status are not only part of Paul's background, but also identifies its role and influence in the formation of a community and community life. In the Greco-Roman cities within the social, political life, economic life, honor, and status were considered as important aspects in conceptions about city and community.[184] The exhortation is directed to love and mutual acceptance in order to avoid division and conflict as the community of believers exist in the midst of the society that emphasizes on status and honor. Paul's exhortation in Romans 12 on community life reflects the morals and virtues of the larger social context that surrounded the believers in Christ. In Romans 12:3-13 Paul warns the believers in Christ in Rome against the desire for honor. Then from Romans 12:14-21 Paul is addressing the community of believers in relating to the people outside the Christian faith community and then connects it with Romans 13:1-7.

Halvor Moxnes reads Paul's exhortation in Romans 12-13 within the context of the honor-shame motif. However, the problem lies in connecting Paul's teaching in Romans 12 with the emphasis on opposing those who think highly of oneself (Rom. 12:3), and the exhortation on being subjects to governing authorities (Rom. 13:1-7). A quick look at Romans 12-13 we find contradictions as Paul's exhortation in Romans 12 denounces the honor system and in Romans 13 Paul accepts the honor system practiced in Roman society. Another rendering is by Neil Elliott, who states that Paul accepted the honor system in the public

---

[184] Halvor Moxnes, "The Quest for Honor and the Unity of the community in Romans 12 and in the Orations of Dio Chrysostom," *Paul in his Hellenistic Context*, Troels Engberg-Pedersen (Edinburgh: T&T Clark, 1994), 203-204.

arena, but renounced it in the private arena within the community of the believers in Christ. Elliott also argues that the language of submission and fear in Romans 13:1-7 is an "exception to the rhetoric of the rest of the letter" where the obedience of God can be summed in the obligation to love one another (Rom. 13:8-11).[185] Elliott's view that Paul's exhortation on the honor system can be a reflection of two different arenas, i.e., the public and the private arena is also probable, yet nowhere in Romans 12-13 do we find such explicit divisions in his exhortations on the honor system. The exhortation in Romans 13:1-7 concerns the external relations of the believers in Christ with the Roman Empire and its superior authorities in matters concerning status and tax. As such, it is probable that amid the influence and impact of the wider Roman society, Paul exhorts the believers in Christ who are small in number to abide by the state and its policies. The believers do not occupy high positions and offices within the Roman Empire, but are subjects and the general masses. A few could have been wealthy and belonged to the middle class, but others belonged to the *humitiores* group. Therefore, they had to abide and adapt to the social and political requirements of the state. It is also likely that he considers the honor system that was widely practiced in the Greco-Roman society and the status-conscious nature of the society and the political policies especially in connection to the tax system. All these points to the understanding that Paul is attentive to the context in which he finds himself. Paul is addressing the believers, but in the context of the internal aspect and the external aspect. Thus, we can conclude that Paul was attentive, especially given the social and political policies of the Roman Empire.

Summary

Thus, from the mentioned spheres in a believer's life we see that a believer in Christ cannot remain completely secluded from the world and the happenings around his/her surrounding. One cannot be exclusively a believer in Christ and do nothing else. Christian faith does not demand from its believers to draw away from the

[185] Elliott, *The Arrogance of the Nations*, 153, 156.

wider sphere, but it calls upon its believing members to participate differently. The Spirit guided relationship thus embraces multiple identities and roles and the believers play their part in their everyday life to the service of God. The multiple identities and roles witness to the glory of God in their common faith as members of the believing community. By embracing multiple identities and roles the believers in Christ can enlarge their boundaries and redefine relationships. This redefinition of relationships occurs in the context of accepting the "other."

Chapter 4

Relational Motif in Romans 15:7-13 and the Claudian Edict

Romans 15:7-13 opens with a call for the members of the Roman believing communities to "accept one another." Paul develops this plea for acceptance on the basis that Christ's ministry is both to the Jews as well as to the Gentiles.[186] The ministry of Christ is God's faithfulness to his promises made to Israel, and God's mercy to the Gentiles. Thus, in this chapter our attention will be on the acceptance motif and Paul's exhortation within the community of the believers in Christ in the light of the Claudian Edict.

Accept One Another (Rom. 15:7)

The Greek word *proslambō* (προσλαμβάνω Rom. 15:7) has a wide spectrum of meanings. It can mean, "to grasp," "to seize," "to exploit," "to take aside," "to receive or extend welcome" or

[186] Brendan Byrne argues that the plea for acceptance points to a "universal glorification" of God [*Romans*, SacPag, Vol. 6. (Collegeville: The Liturgical Press, 1996), p. 428].

"to take along."[187] From the wide spectrum of meanings, two directions in the interpretation of *proslambō* (προσλαμβάνω) emerge. First, the active aspect of the word indicating movement and tension is expressed in "to take" or "to bring." The active aspect especially occurs in the synoptic gospels (Eucharist: Mk. 14:22-23; LK. 24:30,43; Jn. 21:13; Resurrection: Mk. 12:19-22). Second, the less active aspect is expressed in "accept," or "receive" or "acquire."[188] In the New Testament, *proslambō* (προσλαμβάνω) generally occurs in the middle tense. In such occurrences, *proslambō* (προσλαμβάνω) can mean, "to take to oneself" (Acts 18:26; 27:33, 36), "with oneself" (Mk. 8:32), "to receive hospitably" (Philm. 17; Acts 28:2) and "to take in or incorporate all with no inner reservations" (Rom. 14:1-3; 15:7).[189]

In the Pauline epistles, *proslambō* (προσλαμβάνω) occurs only in Romans and Philemon (Rom. 14:1; 15:7; Philm. 17). In Romans, it appears in the context of accepting other people groups and individuals, despite the differences in their ways of life and practices. Likewise, in Philemon, it appears in the context of welcoming into a house. In both contexts, it is a call for incorporating another member or other members in a community or fellowship. Both "accept" and "welcome" can be used interchangeably for *proslambō* (προσλαμβάνω), because as mentioned, it encompasses a wide range of meanings. For Joseph Fitzmyer, *proslambanesthe* (προσλαμβάνεσθε) (Rom. 14:1, 15:7) means, "take to oneself, take into one's household," i.e., "welcome," "accept with an open heart."[190] Likewise, James Dunn suggests that *proslambanesthe* (προσλαμβάνεσθε) (Rom.

---

[187] For details on this term, refer to, Delling, "λαμβάνω, ἀναλαμβάνω, ἀνάλημψις, ἐπιλαμβάνω, ἀνεπίλημπτος, κατα, μεταλαμβάνω, μετάλημψις, παρα-, προ-, προσλαμβάνω, πρόσλημψις, ὑπολαμβάνω,"*TDNT*, ed. Gerhard Kittel, trans. Geoffrey W. Bromiley, vol. 4 (Grand Rapids: WM. B. Eerdmans, 1967), p. 5; *BDAG*, Third edition, p. 833.

[188] See A. Kretzer, "λαμβάνω," *EDNT*, ed. Horst Balz & Gerhard Schneider, vol. 2 (Grand Rapids: William B. Eerdmans, 1991), p. 336; Delling, "λαμβάνω, ἀναλαμβάνω...," p. 5.

[189] Delling, "λαμβάνω, ἀναλαμβάνω...," p. 15.

[190] Fitzmyer, *Romans,* p. 689

14:1, 15:7) means, "Receive or accept into one's society, home, or a circle of acquaintances." He goes on to cite 2 Maccabees 10:15 and Acts 28:2.[191] Mark Nanos also uses both "welcome" and "accept" simultaneously.[192] In the present study, I use the word "accept," for it better conveys the meaning of receiving without having to give up one's way of life, and to grow together as a worshipping community supporting one another.

Paul's exhortation in Romans 15:7-13 begins with a call for acceptance. The double use of *proslambō* (προσλαμβάνω) in Romans 15:7 indicates the importance of the issue. In the first usage (Rom.15:7a), it refers to believers in Christ receiving one another, while in the second usage (Rom.15:7b), it points to Christ's accepting the believers. In Romans 14:1, the strong are to accept the weak, while in the present text with the use of *allēlous* (ἀλλήλους) meaning one another, Paul establishes a more generic reference exhorting the Roman believers in Christ to accept one another (cf. Rom. 12:5, 9-16).

The broadening within a Jew-Gentile setting does not indicate that the hostility between the "strong" and the "weak," concerning Jewish dietary laws and the observance of special days in Romans 14:1-15:6, is resolved or has disappeared. Neither does it demonstrate only that the Jew-Gentile division is the exclusive issue here. Rather, this call for acceptance emphasizes the place of the Gentiles in the covenantal promises.[193] This is latent in the text, as from this point onward, Paul explicates the doctrinal basis, viz., the confirmation of the promises to the fathers (Rom. 15:8) and the glorification of God by the Gentiles because of God's mercy (Rom.15:9a). Furthermore, with the citations from the Jewish Scripture, the status of the Gentiles in the covenant community is justified, where they join the Jews in praising God (Rom. 15:9b-

---

[191] Dunn, *Romans 9-16*, p. 798.

[192] Mark D. Nanos, *The Mystery of the Romans: The Jewish Context of Paul's Letter to the Romans* (Minneapolis: Fortress, 1996), p. 95 (welcome); p. 98 (accept).

[193] Here the discussions are dependent on Dunn, *Romans 9-16*, p. 845.

12) and are made an acceptable offering, sanctified through the Spirit of God (Rom. 15:16).

The issue of diet in a community gathering consisting of both the "weak" and the "strong," appears in Romans 14 (14:2-3, 6b, 14, 20-21). Besides, the cultic imagery in the following verses (Rom. 15:16-17) suggests a worship context. The idea of glorifying God (Rom. 15:7, 8-11) also reflects a liturgical setting. Paul is reminding the Roman believers in Christ of the need to accept one another in the context of community gatherings. Nevertheless, for both groups to accept one another and partake together in common worships and meals, they need to compromise based on strong theological grounding. On the one hand, the Gentiles are not to disregard Jewish dietary habits, but need to be sensitive to them and accommodate their dietary habits accordingly (Rom. 14:13-23). On the other hand, the Jews are not to consider the adherence to the law as an essential prerequisite for Christian faith.

The basis for Paul's exhortation on acceptance is the deed of Christ to the Jews and the Gentiles (Rom. 15:7). This pattern of presenting his exhortation is consistent with Romans 15:1-3a, where Paul's exhortation is based on an appeal to what Christ has accomplished. In these verses, the deed of Christ remains the center of Paul's exhortation. It provides a basis for an important relational motif in Romans 15:7-13 or even in Romans 14-15, i.e., "accept one another."

i. Christ as the Basis for Believers Acceptance (Rom 15:7-8)[194]

Paul refers to the basis for the acceptance with the use of *kathōs* (καθώς) meaning "just as, as, because, since." Scholars are

[194] In this study I have not taken up a detailed study on the syntax and semantics of this text though there are syntactical issues that need attention especially the syntactical relation between Romans 15:8 and 9a. There are solutions proposed by scholars. For details on the syntax and the semantic analysis refer to my previous work, *Acceptance Motif in Romans: Revising Romans 15:7-13* where a complete chapter discuses on the syntactic and semantic analysis and I have also proposed a hypothesis, a reading for the syntactical relation between Romans 15:8 and 9a.

divided on the function of *kathōs* (καθώς) in Romans 15:7. For some scholars, *kathōs* (καθώς) represents a comparative formula, i.e., just as.[195] While others support the rare causal usage of *kathōs* (καθώς), i.e., because/since.[196] The latter use of *kathōs* (καθώς) is to be preferred because it fits better with Paul's way of thinking,

---

[195] For Thompson a comparative καθώς better explains the inclusion of the preposition (εἰς), because "Paul has first prayed that his readers will glorify God (Rom. 15:6) by finding unity in their emulation of Christ" (Michael Thompson, *Clothed with Christ: The Example and Teaching of Jesus in Romans 12:1-15:3*, JSNTSup. 59 (Sheffield: JSOT Press, 1991), p. 230 n.3). Wagner also supports the usual comparative force for it better explain Paul's emphasis on the example of Christ ("The Christ, Servant of Jew and Gentile," pp. 474-475 n.11); J. Ross Wagner, *Heralds of the Good News: Isaiah and Paul "in Concert" in the Letter to the Romans*, NovTSup 101 (Leiden: Brill, 2002), p. 308; Likewise, Joshua D. Garroway translates it "just as," the Roman believers need to welcome one another just as Christ welcomed them ["The Circumcision of Christ: Romans 15:7-13," *JSNT* 34/4 (June 2012): p. 304). See also, Dunn, *Romans 9-16*, p. 846; Fitzmyer, *Romans*, p. 701; Jewett, *Romans*: *A Commentary*, pp. 888-889; Carl N. Toney, *Paul's Inclusive Ethic: Resolving Community Conflicts and Promoting Mission in Romans 14-15*, WUNT 2, Reihe- 252 (Tübingen: Mohr Siebeck, 2008), p. 106; A. Andrew. Das, "'Praise the Lord, All you Gentiles:' The Encoded Audience of Romans 15.7-13," *JSNT*, 34/1 (Sept 2011), p. 91. Strictly speaking, καθώς is a comparative conjunction either suggesting a comparison between two connected ideas or telling about something that needs to be done (Daniel B. Wallace, *Greek Grammer Beyond the Basics* (Grand Rapids: Zondervan Publishing House, 1996), p. 675).

[196] In its causal sense, it especially appears as the conjunction in beginning a sentence (Rom. 1:28; 1Cor. 1:6; 5:7; Eph. 1:4; 4:32; Phil. 1:7) (*BDAG*, Third edition, p. 494). Käsemann is of the opinion that it cannot be a comparative, for it characterizes what follows as eschatological grace for if it is taken as the comparative, then the prepositional phrase at the end would be redundant (Käsemann, *Commentary on Romans*, p. 385). A few others also suggest that it is better to take καθώς in its causal sense and understand the adverb as causative. For, it states the reason for their acceptance of one another and so it cannot be regarded strictly in a comparative sense. Paul is insisting that the Roman believers in Christ should regard one another as members of the family of God. As Christ accepted them so they ought to accept one another. See Cranfield, *Romans*, II: p. 739; Moo, *The Epistle to the Romans*, p. 875; Mark Reasoner, *Strong and Weak. Romans 14:1-15:13 in Context*, SNTS MonographSer. 103 (Cambridge: University Press, 1999), p. 194. Brendan Byrne proposes that the whole phrase beginning with καθώς can be interpreted in either a causal or a

especially in this particular pericope. Comparative use of *kathōs* (καθώς) is improbable for Paul does not seem to be comparing the deed of Christ with that of the believers. Instead, Paul is exhorting the Roman believers to accept one another based on what Christ has done for all. Hence, it is probable that Paul is describing the basis for mutual acceptance. Since Christ has been gracious and accepted everyone, regardless of one's ethnic origin, likewise, the believers in Christ should accept one another, whether the "weak" or the "strong," "Jew" or "Gentile." This reminder to the believers in Christ at Rome is also found in Romans 15:3, 8, where Paul takes up Christ's deed through the use of the word *diakonos* (διάκονος) meaning servant/minister.[197] In the present pericope, the reason for Christ becoming the servant is indicated in the clauses: that Christ might confirm the promises to the fathers consisting in the Gentiles glorifying God for his mercy (Rom. 15:8-9). The use of the perfect[198] infinitive *gegenēsthai* (γεγενῆσθαι – to have become)[199] with *diakonon* (διάκονον –servant/minister) indicates that the role of Christ as the servant from the Jewish origin[200] does not reside in

comparative sense, with the former (cf. Rom. 1:28) having a stronger basis to Paul's reasoning (*Romans*, p. 430).

[197] According to Ernst Käsemann, διάκονος refers to the earthly work of Jesus and it corresponds to the context and the tradition in John 13 (*Commentary on Romans*, p. 385). Along this line, Cranfield suggests that διακονος is the service of Christ as the servant of Yahweh, parallel in meaning to Mark 10:45 and Matthew 20:28 (*Romans*, II: p. 741).

[198] The perfect tense describes an event in the past, whose result exists in the present time. It denotes a past event with an abiding result (Wallace, *Greek Grammar Beyond the Basics*, pp. 573-74).

[199] The aorist tense reading γενέσθαι is supported by the following witnesses: Alexandrian Majuscule (B C*), Western Majuscule (D* F G) and Alexandrian Minuscule (1739. 1881), while the perfect γεγενησθαι is read by Alexandrian Majuscule (ℵ A C²), Western Majuscule (D¹), Alexandrian Minuscule (33) and Byzantine text-type, Majority texts (M). The perfect tense reading is generally accepted, as it is likely that the scribes would alter the perfect tense to the aorist tense then the other way round.

[200] "Servant of circumcised" according to Dunn, *Romans 9-16*, p. 846.

the past alone, but continues in his role as the resurrected Christ.[201] He employs a servant-model (Rom. 15:8): Christ did not please himself (Rom. 15:3). We can, therefore, conclude that with the use of the conjunction *kathōs* (καθώς), Paul is appealing to the pattern of Christ as a motivation for the Roman believers in Christ to accept each other.

In referring to the pattern of Christ, Paul uses *ho Christos* (ὁ Χριστός-Christ with definite article) in Romans 15:7. In the Pauline epistles, *Christos* (Χριστός-Christ without the definite article) and *ho Christos* (ὁ Χριστός-Christ with the definite article) occur without much distinction. But it is highly likely that in this pericope the use of *ho Christos* (ὁ Χριστός) and *Christos* (Χριστός) alternatively in verses 7 and 8 suggest an important differentiation. In Romans 14 and 15, the use of the definite article with *Christos* (Χριστός) is constantly maintained (Rom. 14:18; 15:3, 7).[202] As in Romans 15:3, the definite article in 15:7 indicates that the emphasis of the text is to highlight the significance of *Christos*, the Messiah. Thus, the presence of the definite article *ho* (ὁ) also indicates that *Christos* (Χριστός) needs to be regarded as a title of Jesus, i.e., the Messiah whose deeds benefit both the Jews and the Gentiles.

---

[201] Barrett points that it indicates the state of Christ being a servant who continues to carry out this office [C. K. Barrett, *The Epistle to the Romans* (London: Adam and Charles Black, 1957), p. 271[. This view is also supported by Byrne, *Romans*, p. 431; Cranfield, *Romans*, II: p. 741; Dunn, *Romans 9-16*, p. 847; Jewett, *Romans: A Commentary*, p. 891; Moo, *The Epistle to the Romans*, p. 877; Toney, *Paul's Inclusive Ethic*, p. 107. In contrast, Käsemann follows Ridderboss, suggesting that the perfect tense naturally relates to the result, and not a continuation of the event (Käsemann, *Commentary on Romans*, p. 385). Along this line of argument, Sam Williams adds that Paul does not speak of Jesus' earthly ministry. In addition, he agrees with Ernest Burton in interpreting γεγενησθαι as the "perfect of existing state," where the past act is dropped and the attention is to the existing result. (Sam K. Williams, "Righteousness of God," in Romans," *JBL* 99/2 (1980): p. 287; Ernest De Witt Burton, *Syntax of the Moods and Tenses in New Testament Greek* (Chicago: University of Chicago, 1909), p. 38).

[202] Χριστός preceded with an article in Romans is found in 7:4; 8:35; 9:3,5; 14:18; 15:3, 7, 19; 16:16.

Unlike in Romans 15:7, Christ in 15:8 appears without the definite article *ho* (ὁ), suggesting that it is a proper name. As James Dunn surmises, "The purpose is to focus on the person rather than on the people as the one in and through whom the fulfillment of the covenant promise and gentile incoming has been made possible."[203] Hence, the article *ho* (ὁ) with *Christos* (Χριστός) in Romans 15:7 is significant. After this, Paul reinforces his appeal by referring to the purpose of Christ's acceptance of the believers, i.e., to the glory of God. The purpose of the "glory of God" in Romans 15:7 reflects the Old Testament context of God alone deserving the highest praise and glory (Ps. 149:9; 117:1). Consequently, Romans 15:6-7 becomes the basis for the citations from the Jewish Scripture in Romans 15:9b-12. The catena of citations points to the nations praising and glorifying God.

Scripture Bears Witness to the Call for Acceptance (Rom 15:9b-12)[204]

The function of Scripture in Paul's gospel is reflected both at the very beginning of the Epistle to the Romans when Paul writes, "proclaimed beforehand by God's prophets in the Scripture" (Rom. 1:2), and at the end where he mentions "by the Scripture of the prophets" (Rom. 16:26). Among Pauline epistles, the maximum use of the Old Testament (as a direct quotation, an allusion or ideas, and themes) is found in Romans. The Epistle to the Romans contains a substantial number of quotations and amalgamated citations and chains of citations from the Jewish Scripture, probably because Paul wanted to justify the place of the Jews and the Gentiles in the salvific plan of God. In considering that the letter was an attempt to resolve tensions that divided the Jewish and Gentile believers, Paul may have regarded the authoritative Jewish Scripture as a basis for the common ground for his arguments. This is because his claim as an apostle of Christ

---

[203] Dunn, *Romans 9-16*, p. 846.

[204] For a detailed exegetical analysis of Romans 15:9b-12, refer to my work *Acceptance Motif in Paul: Revisiting Romans 15:7-13*. A complete chapter is dedicated to an analysis of Paul's use of Scripture in Romans 15 within the context of a universal call to praise.

would not have a great impact as he had no prior relationship with the Christian communities in Rome.[205] In this sense, we can say that there is a link between Paul's inclusion of the citations from Scripture and his exhortation on God's acceptance of the Jews and the Gentiles through faith. The citations can thus be considered as a witness to an inclusive community.

i. Witness to an Inclusive Community

In Romans 15:8, Paul refers to the "promises to the fathers," especially in the context of the ministry of Christ to the Jews and the Gentiles. Ross Wagner rightly observes that the catena functions to testify to the purpose of the messiah's ministry in the creation of a community comprising Jews and Gentiles glorifying God together.[206] Paul positions the citation in a manner of presenting the ministry of Christ, the messiah, to the Jews and the Gentiles. In the first scriptural citation (Rom. 15:9b of Ps. 17:50 LXX), the Messiah is presented as one who will confess God among the Gentiles (Rom.15:9b). Paul cites Psalm 17 (LXX) in his exhortation to the Jews and the Gentiles who are to accept one another on the basis that Christ accepted all. In reading David's song as a prefiguration of Christ, we see that it rhymes with the preceding verses where a citation from psalms is put in the mouth of Jesus (Rom. 15:3). Such prefiguration of the psalm is also in line with the Christological context of Romans 15:1-12. Paul refers to the deed of Christ as the basis for Roman believers to accept one another in Romans 15:3. This is explicitly brought out in Romans 15:7 in his call for acceptance. In the next two citations (Rom. 15:11 of Ps. 116:1 LXX and Rom. 15:10 of Deu. 32:43), Christ

[205] This is one possibility out of the three possibilities that Christopher Stanley suggests of why Paul in Romans needed to justify his position with Scripture: First, Scripture was the basis to resolve tensions in the Roman Christian communities. Second, to undo any potential problems that would hinder the support for his mission to Spain. Third, this epistle represents Paul's anticipated audience in Jerusalem, his perception of his appearance before the apostles in Jerusalem (*Arguing with Scripture: The Rhetoric of Quotations in the Letters of Paul* (New York: T&T Clark, 2004, pp. 143-144).

[206] Wagner, *Heralds of the Good News*, pp. 310-11.

extends the invitation to both the Jews and the Gentiles to praise God. The reason for praise by the Jews and the Gentiles harkens back to Paul's exhortation in Romans 15:8-9a, which is about the deed of Christ for all. The last citation in v. 13 (Isa.11:10) speaks of the Messiah in whom the Gentiles will hope. This reading of Christ in Romans 15:7-12 presents a more balanced construction of Paul's exhortation: since Christ has accepted both the Jews and the Gentiles by breaking down the walls of disparity and narrowing the gap between them, so the Roman believers are also called to put away their differences and accept one another based on Christ's ministry. Furthermore, this same Christ gives praise to God amid the Gentiles and is one on whom the Gentiles hope, thus creating space for both the Jews and the Gentiles to glorify God. The service of Christ is to the Jews and the Gentiles. God's purpose is to confirm His promises made to the Jews (Rom. 15:8), in that the Gentiles glorify God for his mercy (cf. Rom. 11:29-30). Therefore, both the Jews and the Gentiles have a reason to praise God (Rom. 15:8-9a). This concept receives support with the citations from the Jewish Scripture, where both the Jews and the Gentiles give glory to God (Rom. 15:9b-11).

ii. A Collective Call to Praise

The content of the catena of citations in Romans 15:9b-12 suggests that Paul is not randomly trying to fit different texts of Scripture together to justify his arguments. Rather, the citations point to a sequence of thought. The different aspects that point to a sequence of thought in Romans 15:9b-12 are discussed below.

Introductory Formula

Romans 15:9b	*kathōs* ***gegraptai*** (καθὼς **γέγραπται**)	Just as it is written
Romans 15:10	***kai palin*** *legei* (**καὶ πάλιν** λέγει)	And again it says
Romans 15:11	***kai palin*** (**καὶ πάλιν**)	And again
Romans 15:12	***kai palin*** *Isaias legei* (**καὶ πάλιν** Ἠσαΐας λέγει)	And again Isaiah says

As the chart shows, all four quotations in Romans 15:9b-12 begin with the usual Pauline customary introductory formula in opening a citation or a catena of citations. In this regard, Scott Hafemann observes Paul's argument in verses 9b-12 as one long continuous argument, with four stages, the last three introduced with *kai palin legei* (καὶ πάλιν λέγει – and again it says) (cf. similar use of *palin* {πάλιν–again} in 1 Cor. 3:20). He explains it by referring to "the switch in verbs from *graphō* (γράφω - write) in verse 9b to *lego* (λέγω – I say) in verses 10-12, the subsequent threefold repetition of *kai palin legei* (καὶ πάλιν λέγει – and again it says) in verses 10-12, and the unpacking of the perfect tense in verse 9b *gegraptai* (γέγραπται – it is written) by the present tenses in the introductory clause of verses 10-12 *legei* (λέγει – it says)."[207] Against this conclusion, Leander E. Keck claims that the introductory form "*kai palin*" (καὶ πάλιν – and again) distinguishes the citations one from the other and they do not form a single "passage" as in Romans 3:10-18.[208] However, Keck fails to explain the reason for asserting that *kai palin* (καὶ πάλιν – and again) differentiates the citations.

As indicated in the chart, the catena of citations opens with *kathōs gegraptai* (καθὼς γέγραπται – as it is written) in Romans 15:9b. This formula *kathōs gegraptai* (καθὼς γέγραπται) indicates the authority of Scripture in the exhortation to the Jews and the Gentiles by linking the catena of citations to the exhortation in Romans 15:7-9a. All citations are linked with *kai palin* (καὶ πάλιν – and again), indicating the same subject is being discussed. For, as pointed out above, *palin* (πάλιν–again) is a marker to show similar nature. Given the citation formula *gegraptai* (γέγραπται-it is written) that opens the catena, the subject attached to *legei* (λέγει –it says) would probably be *he graphē* (ἡ γραφή - the scripture/

---

[207] Scott Hafemann, "Eschatology and Ethics. The Future of Israel and the Nations in Romans 15:1-13," *Tyndale Bulletin*, 51/2 (2000), p. 174.

[208] Leander E. Keck, "Christology, Soteriology, and the Praise of God (Romans 15:7-13)," *The Conversation Continues: Studies in Paul and John. In Honor of J. Louis Martyn*. Edited by Robert T. Fortna & Beverly R. Gaventa (Nashville: Abingdon Press, 1990), p. 91.

writing). It is only in the last citation that the book of Scripture is specified as "Isaiah."

Logical Progression

Most interpreters refer to the "Gentiles" as the word that links the citations.[209] However, a few also include the praise language.[210] The common element in all the citations is indeed the catchword "Gentiles." However, the way the citations are presented may indicate another crucial theme. Noteworthy is Paul's appeal to three parts of the Scripture, viz., the Law, the Prophets, and the Writings, along with the use of diverse praise vocabularies. The praise language is elucidated with parallel terms as given in the chart below.

Praise language		
Romans 15:7	*eis* ***doxan*** *tou Thou* (εἰς **δόξαν** τοῦ θεοῦ - to [the] glory of God) (note that this verse is not a citation, added for reference to show the praise language that dominates in this text).	Glory
Romans 15:9b	*ta de ethnē huper eleous* ***doxasai*** *ton Theon* (τὰ δὲ ἔθνη ὑπὲρ ἐλέους **δοξάσαι** τὸν θεόν – but the Gentiles on behalf of mercy glorify God).	To glorify
Parallel terms		

[209] Murray, *The Epistle to the Romans*, p. 206; Fitzmyer, *Romans*, p. 705; Keck, "Christology, Soteriology, and the Praise of God (Romans 15:7-13)," p. 91; Barrett, *The Epistle to the Romans*, p. 272.

[210] Douglas Moo makes a passing reference that the praise language does connect the citations, but he does not explicate how it binds the citations or even links the citations to the entire pericope (*The Epistle to the Romans*, p. 878).

Romans 15:9b	*dia touto* ***exomologēsomai*** *soi en ethnesin kai tō onomati sou* ***psalō*** (διὰ τοῦτο **ἐξομολογήσομαί** σοι ἐν ἔθνεσιν καὶ τῷ ὀνόματί σου **ψαλῶ**– because of this I will confess you among nations and sing of your name).	Praise Sing
Romans 15:10	***euphranthēte****, ethnē, meta tou laou autou* (**εὐφράνθητε**, ἔθνη, μετὰ τοῦ λαοῦ αὐτοῦ - rejoice, gentiles, with his people).	Rejoice
Romans 15:11	*kai* ***epainesatōsan*** *auton pantes hoi laoi* (καὶ **ἐπαινεσάτωσαν** αὐτὸν πάντες οἱ λαοί - and praise him all the peoples).	Give praise

The first citation (Ps. 17:49 LXX) bears a note of confession in which the psalmist praises God among the Gentiles. Here, David exalts the name of God for delivering him from the hands of his enemies. The second citation (Deu. 32:43 LXX) is an invitation for the Gentiles to rejoice with Israel. The third citation (Ps. 116:1 LXX) emphasizes the universality of praise. The fourth citation (Isa. 11:10 LXX) speaks of the cause of the inclusion of the Gentiles, and the reason for the Jews and the Gentiles for praising God. The references to the Davidic lineage and kingship in Psalm 17:49 (LXX) and Isaiah 11:10 in the first and the last citation of Romans 15:9b-12 provide the basis for the call to praise from Deuteronomy 32:43 and Psalm 116:1 (LXX). In Romans 15, the praise of David is prefigured in Christ, who exalts the name of God for manifesting His power in and through his life. The resurrected Christ exalts the name of God among the nations. As a response to this exaltation, the Gentiles join the Jews in praising God, as indicated in the second citation from Deuteronomy 32:43. The inclusion of the Gentiles results in common praise of the

Jews and the Gentiles in the citation from Psalm 116:1 (LXX). The reference to *hoi laoi* (οἱ λαοί - the people) can be generalized as neither Jew nor Gentile. The psalm emphasizes the collective glorification of God. The cause for this collective praise is the messiah from the "shoot of Jesse" who will restore Israel and on whom the Gentiles will hope.

We can plausibly say that the theme of glory and praise is used to bring different groups together. Two implications arise from this. First, the believers' coming together glorifies God. Second, the believers' coming together is ultimately what God wants. Thus, the language of praise in this pericope contributes to the acceptance of one another in a community comprising the Jews and the Gentiles. The scriptural citations from the Writings, the Law, and the Prophets demonstrate that the whole of Scripture bears witness to God's faithfulness and mercy to the Jews and the Gentiles, resulting in collective praise. The collective call to praise redefines boundaries within the community of the believers in Christ.

Redefining Boundaries

A call for a community comprising of both Jews and Gentiles is especially indicated in Paul's call for acceptance in Romans 15:7-13. In this call for acceptance, Paul urges the Jews and the Gentiles to be open to one another. Consequently, the exclusive claim of the Jews as the only race chosen by God is relativized. Moreover, the meaning of Israel in its strict sense as referring to an ancestor, land, or descent from the tribe of the patriarch is also enlarged upon (Acts 2:36; 7:41; Rom. 9:27; 2Cor. 3:7; Phil. 3:5; Heb. 8:8; Judith 6:2; 3 Esdras 1:30).[211] Such redefinition arises from the act of God in Christ. A brief analysis of Paul's exhortation to the identity of the believers would give us a clearer picture.

Before Romans 9, Paul frequently refers to "Jew and Gentile," but from Romans 9-11 there is a shift in the terminology to "Israel" (Rom. 9:6b). James Dunn argues that Paul is not trying to merge

[211] H. Kuhli, " Ἰσραήλ," *EDNT*, vol. II (Grand Rapids, MI: William B. Eerdmans, 1991), pp. 202-204.

two distinct identities, "Jew and Gentile," but through the shift in terminology to "Israel" Paul opens up a "different possibility." The term "Jew" or "Jews" represents an ethnic identifier or has a geographical connotation. It refers to Jewish people to distinguish them from the other nations. The term "Israel," on the other hand, connotes an "insider" perspective, connected with the covenant. Dunn concludes that "Jew" is understood with the land, whereas "Israel" is understood within the sphere of a believer's relation to God. Nevertheless, it is possible to include "Gentiles" within "Israel" and this is what Paul is attempting to do in Romans 9-11 with the shift in terminology.[212] In the new identity, Israel is not defined by physical descent, but with the divine call. The Greek word *kaleō* (Καλεω̃ - I call, Rom. 9:6-29) is the key word for determining Israel's identity.[213] Such a definition is also taken up in Romans 11:28-29. The children of God are therefore the children of promise and not children of the flesh. Neither is election determined by works, but by God's calling (Rom. 10-13).

The boundary of historical Israel is redefined and this arises from God's salvific act in Christ. In defining the identity of Israel through the call of God, Paul does not deny the election of historic Israel, but redefines it,[214] not by physical descent (Rom. 9:7-12), but through life in Christ. Life in Christ is not a label of identity, but for Israel and the other nations it is a description of belonging. Thus, the coming together of the Jews and the Gentiles remains an important dimension in Paul's emphasis on the theme "in Christ." Paul even states that the example of Christ in accepting all actualizes a collective call to praise (Rom. 15:7-12). For Paul, the promises of God to the fathers are confirmed and actualized in Christ (Rom. 15:7-8). The act of faithfulness actualized in Christ opens up belonging to the Gentiles, who

---

[212] James D. G. Dunn, *The Theology of Paul the Apostle* (Grand Rapids, MI: William B. Eerdmans, 1998), pp. 506-514.

[213] So also, Johann D. Kim, *God, Israel, and the Gentiles. Rhetoric and Situation in Romans 9-11*, SBL Dissertation Series 176 (Atlanta: SBL, 2000), p. 126.

[214] As also, Dunn, *The Theology of Paul the Apostle*, pp. 510, 514.

through mercy praise God along with the Jews (Rom. 15:9-12). They too become worshippers of the God of Israel through the act of Christ. However, the actualization of the promises through Christ does not make them "Israel," in terms of an ethnic group. It rather provides them a new status as children of God.

Paul proceeds to show how in this redefinition the promises of God to the fathers are not nullified. For him, the covenant promises to Israel remain valid and he has frequently emphasized the priority of the Jews in Romans (Rom. 1:16; 2:9, 10; 3:9, 29; 9:24; 15:7). This priority remains because of God's promises to their ancestors (Rom. 11:28-29). The inclusion of the Gentiles does not nullify God's promises to Israel. For, if God's promises were nullified, then the salvation to the Gentiles would have no guarantee. Thus, Paul in Romans 15:8-9a shows that God in Christ remains faithful to the promises to the fathers, but at the same time extends his mercy to the Gentiles, who look up to the Jewish Messiah as a banner (Rom. 15:12). In this sense, the divine act of God in Christ to the Jews and the Gentiles in accepting all redefines the boundary of Israel. This relationship becomes evident and is expressed in a community comprised of believers who wanted to adhere to the Jewish way of life and those who wanted freedom from it.

In redefining the identity of the people of God as being linked to the life in Christ, Paul does not demand the Jews and Gentiles to renounce their ethnic identities as Jews and Gentiles. The identity as people of God adds to the believer's multiple identities and roles as seen in the preceding chapter. To be sure, Paul does not directly use words like "multiple identities" and "roles" concerning the believers in Christ. However, the idea that as followers of Christ, believers continue to belong to the world and participate in the public and private spheres is conspicuous in the Epistle to the Romans. The notion of embracing multiple identities and roles is also emphasized in Paul's call for acceptance in Romans 14-15. He asks neither party to renounce its practices, nor to judge the other. Instead, he calls for acceptance (Rom. 15:7). He exhorts the "strong" to accept the "weak in faith" (Rom. 14:1) and not to despise them (Rom. 1:3). Conversely, the "weak" is not to judge the "strong" (Rom. 14:10). In accepting each other, they can strengthen one another and grow together as a community of faith (Rom. 14:19; 15:2, 5, 7). This leads inexorably to the redefining of their relationship, not based on strict Jewish practices, but through the act of Christ.

Acceptance Motif and the Claudian Edict

As discussed in chapter two of this study, opinions differ on the audience of Romans between the Jewish believers as a majority and the Gentile believers as a majority. However, we cannot propose with certainty a clear-cut division, but can only suggest (as indicated in chapter two) that both Jewish and Gentile believers are referred to, in the epistle to the Romans. In considering the edict of Claudius expelling the Jews from Rome in AD 49 as a possible historical background for Paul's letter to the Romans, it could have considerably molded the early years of Christian faith in Rome (as discussed in chapter two). After the expulsion of AD 49, the Gentiles took over most of the key positions in the home-gatherings. We can probably agree with James Dunn that Aquila and Priscilla demonstrated their leadership qualities in the "intra-Jewish debates in Rome" before their expulsion in AD 49.[215] The return of the Jews with the death of Claudius (AD 54) also included Jewish believers in Christ, like Aquila and Priscilla, Andronicus and Junia, and others (Rom. 16). In such a situation where the home-gatherings were predominantly Gentile, it would have been difficult for the Jewish believers to regain their leadership roles. The Jewish believers also had to identify with the Gentile home-gatherings that separated themselves from the synagogue.[216] With the return of the expelled Jewish believers in Christ who wanted to uphold the Jewish ways of life, there were tensions among the believers in Christ in Rome. In such a

---

[215] James D. G. Dunn, *The Acts of the Apostles* (Peterborough: Epworth press, 1996), p. 241.

[216] Dunn, *Romans1-8*, p. liii.

context, Paul in Romans 15:7-13 brings an important relational motif, that is, the notion of acceptance. Paul reminds the believers in Christ that it is important to accept one another and to build each other as a community, in order to avoid any uproar that will attract the attention of the Roman authorities. Before the expulsion the believers in Christ worshipped together with the Jews in the Synagogues and the Roman authorities did not really distinguish between the Jews and the Christian faith. The Jews had certain concessions with regard to worship, rituals, and practices within the empire because of their long history of faith and tradition. However, after the believers in Christ broke ties and separated from the Synagogues, it would have been evident to the Roman authorities that Christian faith was different from the Jewish faith, and this would have called for close monitoring and observation by the authorities. As a result, Paul did not want the Christian faith communities to have any negative impact within the wider society through their practices, behaviors, and attitudes. Furthermore, Paul also had a missional agenda as he wanted to take the gospel of Christ as far as Spain, and for this he wanted the corporation and help of the Roman believers. Therefore, he wanted the Roman believers in Christ to maintain cordial relations among themselves and also with the larger society. As such, he exhorts the believers in Christ comprising of both Jews and Gentiles to accept each other amidst their diverse ethnic and traditional backgrounds.

Summary

The call for acceptance is on the basis of the example of Christ who accepted both the Jews and the Gentiles to the glory of God, and to this, Scripture also bears witness. The gospel he proclaims and his mission are presented in continuity with Scripture. Noteworthy is Paul's strategy of interweaving texts from the Law, Prophets, and Writings in a closely knitted structure in order to indicate that the acceptance of the Gentiles is found within the key cluster of Scripture. This powerfully provides an avenue for both the Jews and the Gentiles to glorify God together.

Hence, the citations are not only connected to each other, but are interpreted within the context of the deed of Christ and they serve as support for Paul's exhortation in Romans 15:7-9a. In this sense, they unpack the significance of the ministry of Christ to the Jews in his faithfulness to his promises and to the Gentiles in showing mercy. This, in turn supports the call for the Roman believers in Christ to accept one another on the basis that Christ has accepted everyone to the glory of God. Thus, having demonstrated the place of the catena of citations in support of Paul's exhortation within the context of the ministry and the deed of Christ in his call for acceptance in Romans 15:7-13, we now turn to the interpretive framework for redefining relationships in the subsequent chapter.

Chapter 5

An Interpretive Framework for Redefining Relationships in Romans

The preceding chapters had made an attempt to situate Romans within its historical and social context. Thus, having examined Romans 12-13 and 15:7-13 closely within the said context, we will develop an interpretive framework for redefining relationships within the community of the believers in Christ and also with the wider society, including the imperial setting.

Interpretive Framework

From our analysis in the preceding chapters, three aspects can be highlighted in our attempt to redefine relationships: redefining relationships have wider implications, redefining relationships demands obligations, and redefining relationships calls for the need to develop a hermeneutic of love, honor, and hospitality.

i. Redefining Relationships has Wider Implications

From our study, we see that redefining relationships have wider implications. Paul begins with self-renewal by emphasizing on the renewing of the mind; in order that the individual believer's life is holy, good, and well-pleasing to God (Rom. 12:1-2). The primary step in order to redefine one's relationship with God begins with self-knowledge, self-awareness, and self-criticism. So, as seen in chapter three Paul calls his readers to be transformed through their relationship with God, a redefined relationship that is rooted in the virtues of holiness, goodness, acceptable and perfect will of God. Yet, Paul's exhortation does not end with a self-transformed and renewed relationship with God, but it has communal implications. The community relationship is built on personal relationships. Therefore, Paul calls his readers to be sober-minded and connects it with the analogy of the body whose individual members build one another (Rom. 12:3-8) by accepting each other (Rom. 15:7-13). Thus, in the redefined relationship, the common faith of the believers represented in their allegiance to God in Christ becomes the basis for unity and harmonious growth. The common belief in Christ strengthens their bond as a community. Hence, in order to promote and appreciate their common identity in Christ, Paul admonishes against a judgmental and arrogant attitude, as it contradicts his call to accept one another as a community of faith. William Campbell remarks, "*the lifestyle to which their faith commits them is not something about which to boast above other believers*."[217]

The redefining of relationships does not restrict itself within the community of the believers in Christ, but it is extended to include the wider society. This is because Christian faith cannot survive in isolation, as it is part and parcel of the wider society or the universe. Our neighbor does not merely consist of members within the faith community, or someone next door, but it has a wider connotation. For instance, we find in Deuteronomy 24 a broader understanding of neighbors where we do not directly find the usage of the term neighbor, but the idea is present. There are indications to care and leave space for people who are to come after us, someone we have never encountered. The Deuteronomic

[217] William S. Campbell, *Unity and Diversity in Christ: Interpreting Paul in Context. Collected Essays* (Eugene, Oregon: CASCADE Books, 2013), p. 65.

law in 24:19-22 clearly remarks that specific parts need to be un-harvested for the poor. It is clear that even in the case of an unknown person our responsibility stands. The concern is protecting the rights and privileges of sojourners, orphans, and widows in Ancient Israel. This Law is also visible in the story of Ruth where she is an alien, an orphan, and a widow, and Boaz orders his workers to leave a handful of grains for Ruth to gather (Ruth 2:16). In the Old Testament times, the landowners were obliged to leave behind some food and grain unharvested so that those in need can meet their needs from them. This practice kept the needy from the humiliation of begging for subsistence, though the field owner did not get any profit out of it.[218] It was simply rendering help on humanitarian ground as co-creatures of God. Likewise, in the parable of the Samaritan in Luke 10:29-37 the focus is on the command of loving a neighbor. Gordon Wenhem comments "Love and neighbors are wide rangers in their scope and meaning in Hebrew as corresponding English terms."[219] In the Old Testament love and neighbor or concern and neighbor generally correspond to one another. So also, in the New Testament whenever the question of who is my neighbor is raised, then automatically the debate on the commandment of love also comes. Like in Paul, the commandment to love one's neighbor is to fulfill the whole law (Gal. 5:14). Thus, the concept of neighbor in the Bible is not only a reference to those in close proximity. Any human being by virtue of his/her being a creature of God is a neighbor. The believers in Christ are encouraged to live peaceably with all by extending the good works and hospitality outside the boundary of the family or close-knit communities (Rom. 12:17-21). The teaching on building relationships and redefining it outside our closed boundaries is on the basis of the ethic of love (Rom. 13:8-

---

[218] Duane L. Christensen, *Deuteronomy 21:10-34:12,* WBC Vol. 6B (Nashville: Thomas Nelson Publishers, 2002), pp. 597-598.

[219] Cited by Richard S Hess, "rea" in *New International Dictionary of Old Testament Theology and Exegesis, vol. 3*, Edited by Willem A. VanGemeren (Grand Rapids, Michigan: Zondervan Publishing House, 1997), p. 1146.

10). This ethic becomes a basis for redefining relationships with the wider society.

In the Epistle to the Romans, Paul's call for redefining relationships is not to be interpreted as a call for the renunciation of prior identities and roles. It is not about giving up one's cultural and ethnic identity after becoming a believer in Christ. Instead, it is about redefining the believer's relationship with God, with fellow beings within the community of the believers in Christ and with the wider social context.

As mentioned, Paul does not explicitly employ words like "multiple identities" and "roles" in his exhortations. Nonetheless, from this study we can conclude that Paul in Romans 12-13 and Romans 15:7-13 reminds the believers in Christ of their diverse identities and roles as members of the believing community and as belonging to the larger world. These diverse roles help in connecting and relating to one another and to the other.

ii. Redefining Relationships Demands Obligations

In the Epistle to the Romans, there are a few explicit references to the notion of obligation.[220] As discussed in chapter three, these references, especially in Romans 13 can be understood in relation to the Roman law of obligations, especially within the context of the honor system. As discussed in the preceding chapters, in Roman society, the morality of obligation can be seen in the exposition of terms like *officium* (duty) and *beneficium* (gift-giving). While it is likely that the obligation described is mainly in the context of the elite in Rome where exchanges occurred between people of equal status, nevertheless, it can function as well within the wider Roman society. As also discussed in chapter two, Patronage was an important aspect of social relationships in Roman society; it is personal in nature and it defined relationships between people of unequal status. Apart from Roman society, scholars also detect patronage in early Christian writings.[221]

---

[220] Romans 1:14; 8:12; 11:35; 13:8; 15:1; 16:2.

[221] Some examples are how John K. Chow applies patronage and "social-networks" to 1 Corinthians [*Patronage and Power: A Study of Social Networks*

Likewise, 1 Clement 38.2 points to obligation within the church and employs the language of reciprocity. Hence, it is possible that there existed some form of reciprocity in the relationships within the early Christ believing communities. Given this understanding of obligation among believers in Christ, it is not inconceivable to consider Paul's exhortations in Romans within such a setting (as discussed in chapter three).

The notion of obligation in Romans is in the context of the believing communities. The believers are called to be obligated to one another in love and this also applies to their relationship towards those outside the Christian faith communities and the superior authorities (Rom. 12-13). Paul demonstrates the life of faith. This life, William Campbell observes is a "life of commitment rather than of vacuous freedom, of obligation to Christ and to other humans."[222]

In this study, the discussion on obligation within the Roman Christian faith communities fit Mark Reasoner's application of the obligation and the ethic of reciprocity as Paul's solution to the problems of the "weak" and the "strong." Reasoner suggests that Paul used the social forces bound up in patronage for the communities and fits it with the love command. In this regard, Reasoner observes that in Romans 14:1-15:13, Paul's argument presents a progression on the notion of obligation, which includes the "element of reciprocity."[223] However, this study will consider Paul's call for acceptance as an obligation for the believers on

---

in Corinth, JSNTSup. 75 (Sheffield: JSOT, 1992)]. G. W. Peterman applies social reciprocity to Philippians [*Paul's gift from Philippi: Conventions of Gift Exchange and Christian Giving*, SNTSMS 92 (Cambridge: Cambridge University Press, 1997)].

[222] Campbell, *Unity and Diversity in Christ: Interpreting Paul in Context*, p. 61.

[223] For discussion on the progression, see Mark Reasoner, *The Strong and the Weak*, pp. 187-199. Gerd Theissen in his title *The Social Setting of Pauline Christianity: Essays on Corinth* (Philadelphia, PA: Fortress Press, 1982), pp. 138-140, takes up the issues of obligation, especially the "love-Patriarchalism" in the context of Corinth, but he does not incorporate the ethic of reciprocity that we find in the Roman context.

the basis of Christ's acceptance of all. Paul begins with social obligations that the members owe to one another (Rom. 14:1-4; 14:13-15:3; 15:7). The "strong" are obligated to accept the "weak" (Rom. 14:1-3) and the "weak" are obligated not to judge the "strong," neither the "strong" are to judge the "weak" (Rom. 14:3, 4, 13) because every individual believer has a distinct relationship with God. This suggests that judging one another is taking the place of God as the judge (Rom. 14:4). It is to God alone that all believers are accountable. In their personal faith relationship, individuals are thankful for the act of Christ and fulfill their obligation toward the deity. This obligatory act, which is already practiced toward the deity, is used by Paul to bring the groups to perform it at the community level, where the members unite and glorify God together.[224]

Thus, the primary obligation in giving thanks and glory to God is accomplished in the present obligation of accepting one another within the believing communities in Rome. The present obligation of social harmony according to Mark Reasoner is fulfilled, by "remembering the eschatological obligation to glorify God."[225] The obligation to give thanks and glory to God is on the basis of divine benefits through the deed of God in Christ (Rom. 6:12-8:39), and also with the thought of future benefits in the immediate life and the final stage of life. The obligatory gratitude occurs in the hope for further benefactions, i.e., the hope of return benefits.[226] However, this obligation to glorify God cannot be accomplished if a believer thinks of oneself more highly than one ought to think (Rom. 13:3), or through superior attitude in judging one another (Rom. 14-15), but only in their coming together as a faith community. They are obligated to love and to share a special relationship with Christ. The obligation in relation to this relationship of accountability prohibits pronouncing judgment on

---

[224] For the line of argument in this section, see also Reasoner, *The Strong and the Weak*, pp. 190-191.

[225] Reasoner, *The Strong and the Weak*, p. 191.

[226] Reasoner, *The Strong and the Weak*, pp. 193-194.

the other believer and calls for the acceptance of one another as all are accountable to God in Christ.

Paul's emphasis on "common obligation"[227] in giving what is due to one another and in accepting one another can result in peaceful coexistence among the members of the community of believers in Christ and also with the wider society and the superior authorities. The obligation toward one another is based on the relationship between believers and Christ (Rom. 15:7). Hence, the relationship between believers and Christ impacts the relationship between members of the believing community and the wider society. As the saving act of Christ extends to the Jews as well as the Gentiles, this activity through the saving work of God in Christ is presented as a basis for the obligation (Rom. 14:9; 15:3; 15:8-12). Paul's call for acceptance thus demands a mutual obligation, and since the basis for being obligated to accept one another is rooted in a divine-human relationship, this then results in the redefinition of relationships. The redefining of relationships in the individual, community, social, and civil spheres also helps in understanding Paul's emphasis on the ethical values of love, honor, and hospitality.

iii. The Need for a Hermeneutic of Love, Honor, and Hospitality

It is important to develop a hermeneutic of love, honor, and hospitality because the Pauline community at Rome needed to redefine relationships on grounds that it was a community of Jews and Gentiles; that the believers in Christ who were expelled during the time of Claudius had recently returned and that the faith community was also existing within the context of the larger Roman society.

Paul addresses the believers in Christ in Rome to do God's will in a way that moves beyond the social status, class, prevalent ideologies, cultures, and ethnic groups. A call to move beyond the prevalent social construes is grounded in the will of God. Such a

---

[227] The phrase "common obligation" is used by Mark Reasoner in the exhortation of Paul in accepting one another (*The Strong and the Weak*, p. 194).

call within the Roman community of believers in Christ, grounded on "love, honor, and hospitality" create "space" for diverse roles and participation that overlaps in the context of community formation. The Bible and tradition are a call for love, honor, and hospitality and Paul in his ethical exhortation to Roman believers in Christ emphasizes these virtues.

The motif of love is given importance in Romans with the constant reference to practicing genuine love within the community. The social obligations that believers in Christ are obligated within the Roman society or their patron within the social context become subordinate to the pressing debt of love within the believing community.[228] Through the emphasis on the need to practice brotherly/sisterly love, the Roman believers in Christ are reminded of the importance of loving God and doing his will and also loving one another and living peaceably among themselves and with the larger society outside the faith community. It is not a love that is expressed out of pity or to gain a name, instead, Paul is referring to genuine and un-assumed love. A brotherly/sisterly love (Rom. 12:10) is a love expecting nothing in return and it is a love shown regardless of status. A love that transforms and builds one another, a love that accepts the "other," a love that makes space for the "other," a love that gives without expecting anything in return, and a love that guarantees a peaceful environment (Rom. 12:9-10; 13:9-10; 15:7).

Further, Paul urges the believers in Christ to take the lead in honoring one another. As indicated in chapter two, the status and honor system was widely practiced in the Roman territory, and as Spencer Elliott observes it is also likely that the Roman believers in Christ would have been familiar with the system. As citizens of Rome or residents of the Roman territory, the believers in Christ would also have been recipients of the public benefaction and in return bestowed the honor to the benefactors. In considering the societal status of the early believers in Christ as also representing the lowest strata of the society like craftsmen and freed slaves or slaves, it is likely that many would have been

[228] Elliott, "Political Paul and the Social Context of Romans 12-13," p. 10.

bound within the patron-client relationship.[229] Thus, for Paul in any context or situation as long as it concerns honor the believers are to esteem the "other" fellow being more highly than himself/herself. In valuing and appreciating one another regardless of cultural, ethnic, socio-economic, and religious background, we make space for openness to accept one another and build positive and transformative relationships.

Finally, Paul exhorts the believers in Christ to practice hospitality. From our reading of the text in Romans 12-13 Paul uses the root word *philoxenia* for hospitality. This word literally means "love of a stranger." As seen in the interpretation, it appears together with the verb "to receive, accept, take with the hand, or embrace." Thus, hospitality is not just a narrow understanding of feeding someone or giving temporary shelter to someone. Hospitality is not just about being nice but has a wider connotation. It also includes being just. So, therefore it calls for the need to listen, appreciate, and acknowledge more openly the critical voices in our midst. It is making space for people we do not really know, people outside our families and communities, it is making room for people to be accepted, to feel loved, to stand for their cause and embracing them into our community. Christine D. Pohl, on hospitality also makes a similar observation, "communities that are best at welcoming people are communities that know who they are. They have a defined identity. They have something to offer. There is a space for the welcome. There are space and identity to welcome people into, and it's a place that people want to be welcomed into." Nevertheless, in welcoming and making space Pohl also notes the tension between hospitality and fidelity that communities have to encounter. Yet, in such a context, she offers a possibility of taking the stand of Jean Vanier, who views

---

[229] Elliott, "Political Paul and the Social Context of Romans 12-13," pp. 7-8. For details on the social status of the early believers in Christ in Rome refer to Peter Lampe, who assumes that many would have been crafts-workers (*From Paul to Valentinus,* p. 50).

that when we welcome people, we ask for minimal conformity and allow maximal space for diversity.[230]

These three motifs, i.e., love, honor, and hospitality are important motifs in Paul's exhortation to the believers in Christ in redefining relationships. The Hermeneutics of love, honor, and hospitality move beyond the closed exclusive community to include people from all walks of life and social standing. Thus, the motifs of love, honor, and hospitality creates space by moving beyond social hierarchies, social status, and privileges prevalent in the Roman society and redefines relationships in the believers' common alliance to God. In their relationship with God, the believers are called to be living sacrifices, holy and acceptable before God. Paul calls for a redefinition of relationships, i.e., transformative (Rom. 12:1-2).

Summary

As a way of summary, we can first point out that redefining relationships has wider implications. Christian faith cannot be practiced or lived out in isolation as it continues to exist within the wider world and therefore it needs to make a transformative and positive impact as a faith community. Second, redefining relationships calls for the obligation. It is built on the basis of the deed of Christ, who accepted both the Jews and the Gentiles. This obligation takes place in the believers' coming together and accepting one another. Third, the incorporation of the motifs of justice, mercy, and faith helps in redefining our relationship with members of the Christian faith communities as well as our attitude and care towards those outside our faith communities.

[230] Christine D. Pohl, "Hospitality, trust and reweaving the fabric of community," https://faith and leadership.com (accessed on December 9, 2019).

Chapter 6

Conclusion

From this study, we learn the following:

1. That the Epistle of Romans reflects the Roman social status, especially the honor-shame nexus and the Roman imperial system and ideologies. Therefore, it also connects the Epistle of Romans to the Edict of Claudius (49 CE) that led to the expulsion of Jews and Jewish Christians, which changed the setting of Christian faith in Rome.
2. That Roman 12-13 is about redefining relationships. In Romans 12-13 we learn that for Paul there are three dimensions of relationships at the personal level, at the Christian faith community level and the level of the wider social and imperial context. By employing multiple identities and roles believers can connect and relate with one another and to those outside the Christian faith communities.
3. That for Paul, the three dimensions of relationships need to be framed by the acceptance motif. The call for acceptance describes a new kind of relationship; a relationship expressed in openness, i.e., an openness to accept the "other." In

accepting one another, relationships are redefined and people move from the narrow boundaries to a larger "sense of the whole." That relationship within the internal circle of Christian faith communities and also the external faith groups and communities outside and the Roman imperial context includes an interpretative framework for redefining relationships. Thus, the study recommends that redefining relationships have a wider implication; it demands obligations and the need for a Hermeneutic of Love, Honor, and Hospitality.

In conclusion, in redefining relationships we can critique the past built walls and to move toward creating space for openness, and appreciating our differences. Christianity does not draw away individual believers from the faith community of believers, the wider sphere of the society, or from their own culture and traditions, but it demands of its members to participate differently. Consistent with Paul's call for acceptance, our multiple identities and roles would continue to persist in life, even after we become Christians, but they would be utilized in the service of God and for "the whole inhabited world."

Appendix

Does Paul Have Anything to Say to us Today?

In Paul we have a model of how to live a Christian life, which is taking the diversity seriously and being attentive to the context. It is redefining the Christian ways of life to what Paul understands the gospel of Christ to be. We can suppose that Paul did not want to go too far in his interpretation, as he had to accept Roman policies. This is probably because, in a Roman dominant context where believers in Christ are a minority, Paul wanted the believers and Christian faith to maintain peaceful coexistence, as the gospel that Paul preached is also about peaceful coexistence and the prince of peace.

The reason for adding this appendix is to try to pursue some of the themes reflected in Romans in the present context. The appendix is included to illustrate how the arguments in the book on Romans 12-13 and 15:7-13 can be deployed in helping readers to understand more fully the issues that confront us in our communities. There is no doubt that the question of application is a large and complex, but necessary task that deserves careful attention. Several general areas can be identified for an interpretation of Paul's call for redefining relationships in the present context/setting for future directions.

Paul articulated the gospel of Christ in ways that were relevant to the church in Rome. The gospel message was designed to help members within the community in relating and connecting with one another and also in connecting to the larger society, as the church is also a part of the wider society and not outside it. Thus, as discussed, Paul's gospel emphasizes on redefining relationships by considering its wider implications. However, the redefining of relationships cannot take place in isolation, neither it is a passive act, nor a one-sided relation, but it demands obligation to one another. It calls for being careful and mindful of one another. It is a call for living out love, honor, and hospitality. Now the question is, what if anything does the redefining of relationships that Paul emphasized in Romans has to say to us today.

Paul's exhortation on redefining relationships in the context of the Jewish and Gentile believers in Christ, and also within the larger society becomes relevant, especially as he emphasizes obligations, acceptance, love, honor, and hospitality. These values are important in our everyday life and in relating to one another, especially in a context where class hierarchies, status, individual name, and honor play an important part, in the context of diverse cultures, faith traditions, ethnic groups, behaviors, and attitudes. It is also relevant in our prevailing context and situations like our response towards destructions and broken humanity in war zones, our response towards migrants and immigrants, our response towards the mother earth, our response towards hunger, poverty, and unemployment and our response to each other and the situation in times of the global pandemic-COVID-19. While such diverse platforms, encounters, and contexts provide an opportunity to appreciate, respect, learn from one another and positively build relations and connect with the other, it also has resulted in being negative towards one another. It led to individuals and groups being over-protective of oneself and one's group leading to the closure of boundaries and space. It has also made us ethnocentric to protect our distinct identities and lifestyles; there is also a tendency to be suspicious of "the other." Today instead of celebrating our diversities, our mistrust prevents us from accepting and being open towards those who do not belong to our respective faith community or ethnic group. This mistrust is at the center of many of the conflicts, atrocities that erupt in communities and society, and even within churches. In such a context, Paul's call for redefining relationships within the believers' community and the wider society provides communities, ethnic groups, and faith groups with a model of appreciation and obligation toward "the other." It provides opportunities to redefine and transform relationships, and hope for a better future.

As mentioned, the goal of this study has not been to contextualize Paul; therefore, we will not go into details of interpreting Paul within the diverse contexts and situations mentioned above. Hence, I want to briefly highlight only two areas to get an idea of how Paul's redefining of relationships has lessons in our present context. First, we will understand Paul's teachings in a tribal and communitarian context regarding the dilemmas posed by class hierarchies, tribalism, and the honor system. For this, we will briefly look into the tribal and the community-based context of the Nagas in Nagaland (a state in Northeast India). Second, we will look into Paul's call for redefining relationships in the context where our world is grappling with the harsh and sad reality of the novel Coronavirus.

Example One: Community-Based Context

We will look into the context of the Nagas in Nagaland as the Naga society is communitarian and the society is multi-cultural, multi-tribal, and multi-lingual.

i. Feast of Merit and honor in the traditional Naga Society

The Nagas are community-oriented, community gatherings and fellowships are given importance and this is visible even today, although we can say that there is also a decline in its importance. The communitarian aspect is also seen in the religious life of the Nagas. To be truly human, for a Naga, is to belong to the whole community extended to the ancestors and the creation, and to participate in the belief, rituals, and festivals in the community.[231]

As a communitarian society the notion of equality by birth existed irrespective of clan and family. In the traditional society the social status and place of the Nagas depended on the ability of a person to provide feasts. From ancient times the chief of the village or the clan was honored and highly respected. Under the administration of the chief there were also rich members of the community who rendered valuable services, material goods, and physical help to the members of the community, especially in times of famine, epidemics, and war. The rich in the community also organized feasts for the community and it was only by sharing their wealth that they gained honor, and prestige. In the case of a poor man, if he had rich relatives or family members, the rich members would organize a feast of merit on behalf of the poor relative to elevate his social status. These were regarded as "feast of merit." For a married man it gave him an opportunity for prestige as well as to compete for status in society. The prestige was tied to the public display of wealth. The number of feasts varied from the tribe and ethnic group. The high status could be achieved only through "feast of merit." It was a social ceremony involving a series of ceremonies and rituals performed by the married man to elevate the social status of his family. These feasts were optional and involved feeding the entire village by slaughtering of animals and drinking rice beer. The feasts were ranked in importance and each feast led to a stage in social ranking. The stages were connected with rights and rank giving access to new kinds of personal adornment related to a status like special kinds of cloths, shawl, ornaments, house decorations, construction of stone structures, and Y-shaped wooden post outside the house of the one giving feasts. By observing the "feast of merit" a man and his wife gained honor in the present life and the life after death. It also brought favor from the spirits to the village, community,

---

[231] Bendangjungshi, *Confessing Christ in the Naga Context: Towards a Liberating Ecclesiology* (Münster: LIT Verlag, 2011). For analogies in Africa, cf. Kwame Gyekye, *African Cultural Values. An Introduction* (Accra, 1996).

and clan to which the man belonged.[232] Thus, we see that in the traditional Naga society a man did not gain social prestige and status by possessing wealth and accumulating it for his family, but only by spending it for the benefit of the community.

Sharing and giving gifts among the family, clan, and members of the same tribe were common in the traditional Naga society. Gift-giving was a reinforcement of the bond among the kin members. It was part of the duties and responsibilities connected to the kinship relationship.[233]

ii. Attitude Towards the Other Members in the Present-day Naga Society

In the present Naga society the practice of the feast of merit is not explicitly visible, but hosting a community feast by individuals and families still play an important part. The well-to-do in the community, church, clan, tribe, and so on host feast on occasions like tribal festivals, Christmas, Easter for a particular community, or church. By hosting such feasts and sharing their wealth with their respective communities they gain honor and prestige in the society. It is not mandatory, but the well-to-do practice it as part of sharing with the community, to which is tied honor and status. In return the members of the community, tribe, and clan and the beneficiaries honor and respect the host family. In the present Naga society the wealthy members, bureaucrats, governing authorities, and their immediate family members are highly respected and honored. Whereas, the less well-to-do or those surviving hand to mouth are less respected, and usually their presence in social,

---

[232] For the feast of merit refer to, Iris Odyuo, "The various aspects of Naga art," *IOSR Journal of Humanities and Social Science*, 9/4, (March-April 2013): 15-16; Shimreichon Luithui, "Naga: A People struggling for self-determination." https//:www.iwgia.org/images/publications//naga.pdf (accessed on March 15, 2020); M. Sashi Jamir, "The Impact of Modernization on the Nagas: Anthropological Analysis and Theological Response," 9-10, A thesis submitted to Asbury Theological Seminary, 2011. https://sashi2jamir.files.wordpress.com/2012/07/the-impact-of-modernization-on-the-nagas1.pdf (accessed on March 15, 2020).

[233] Luithui, "Naga: A People struggling for self-determination."

ecclesial, and family gatherings is taken for granted. Honor and respect in the social, the ecclesial community and family occasions are generally tied to wealth, social standing, profession, and family background.

As mentioned, hence, we see that from the social aspect there is also a strong tendency of tribalism and social status-consciousness. It is a society where wealth and status are tied to respect and honor. Hence, it is important to redefine relationships.

iii. Redefining Relationship

Despite the efforts taken in some contexts in manifesting the relation-building nature, in general, it continues to remain a challenge for the Nagas in Nagaland. Many times a multi-ethnic context instead of seeing the beauty in diverse people groups coming together we are building walls. The problem of being divided based on ethnicity continues to exist. In recent years, time and again we continue to witness conflicts between the tribes. In many instances the individual problems also turn out into tribal conflicts. This shows that tribalism continues to be strongly rooted in the very being of many of our Nagas. By employing the body metaphor in Romans 12 Paul reminds the believers of the importance of acknowledging one another. So also in Romans 15, Paul reminds the believers that in accepting one another, relationships are redefined and transformed. This redefinition of relationships is perceived in an inclusive community of the Jews and the Gentiles in their common faith. The exhortation of Paul's call for accepting one another and redefining boundaries has a decisive implication in a multi-ethnic context.

The competition for status and honor widely existed in the traditional Naga society. In the present day Naga society the "feast of merit" does not exist, but as mentioned, other community feasts like tribal festivals, Christmas, New year, and so on connected to status and honor is widely practiced. A person's place and status in the Naga society is tied to wealth, profession, and family background. As such, honor and respect are also tied to social status and family background. In such a context Paul's call to "take lead" in honoring one another becomes important. As visible in Paul's exhortation, the honor should not be tied to social status, but believers in Christ are expected to esteem "other" more highly than themselves.

Example Two: COVID-19: Fear, Anxiety, and Challenges

Today the world is battling the novel Coronavirus (COVID-19). The virus that is reported to have its outbreak in China, has made its way far and wide. It is a global phenomenon with intense consequences. It has traveled at a very rapid speed with harsh impacts upon the continents, and countries. The interconnected and dependent nature of our world today has created pathways for the virus to reach far and wide. This virus affects all people, rich and poor, high class or low class, advanced nations, developing nations, and under-developed nations, all ethnic and racial groups, religions, and rural and urban areas. It affects all sectors of life, the health care sector, economy, social life, religious life, education, family and individual income, mental health, well-being, and the list can go on. Today we are encountering a virus that knows no boundaries and affects and infects people from all walks of life and therefore all measures are being taken to stop it. Medical experts are putting together their findings and sharing their updates to develop vaccines. But, how long will it take? No definite answers that we will get as of now.

The novel Coronavirus has locked humans down in their homes or within their locality, countries, cities, and towns and it has closed borders. While many have the luxury to call home/ house, maintain social distancing and stay safe, there are many for whom a home means the pavements, roadsides, public spaces, or for many who lives in slums and refugee camps, social distancing and staying safe is a far cry. However, amid fear, anxiety, and challenges this pandemic poses, we hear encouraging stories from around the world. We hear stories of reaching out to one another, stories of sharing with the needy, stories of helping out where help is needed, stories of risking life to care and treat those sick, stories of those working behind the scene to keep our surroundings healthy and clean, to provide with the essentials, to keep the city/town/community under control, and so on. Every day we hear of encouraging and reassuring stories of helping, relating, and connecting during the pandemic. The contributions of the people around the globe irrespective of their community, nation, race, ethnic groups, religions are appreciated and the world community continues to learn from one another and grow together during the global pandemic crises.

Nonetheless, despite the efforts taken in many contexts in manifesting the relation-building nature, in general, it continues to remain a challenge for many around the globe. Amid the challenges to protect human health, we are faced with other challenges related to human dignity and respect. There is fear, anxiety, grief, poverty, insecurity, xenophobia, loneliness, depression, suspicion, blame game, and the list can go on. Since the emergence of the COVID-19 pandemic, we have heard about and witnessed instances of xenophobia, stigmatization, stereotyping, blame game, and widespread poverty. Stigmatization results in misinformation, the discrimination of the vulnerable groups and it triggers racism and xenophobia. This stops us from moving forward and puts us all at risk as many would start hiding even when infected by the virus because of the stigma attached to it. Stigmatization is a dreadful virus because it stops us from combating the pandemic together. The pandemic is also likely to force millions of people into extreme poverty around the globe. The measures taken to contain the spread of the pandemic are affecting families and households in different ways like job loss, high price, less or no income, disruption of health care services and education, and so on. There is also a challenge to force people to stay at home without working, especially in the case of daily wage workers. The poor are the ones who are hit the hardest by the pandemic, as they do not have the luxury to work from home and get paid.

The panic in the times of the pandemic is also stirred by unreasonable behavior, attitude, and actions of many people. Xenophobia has intensified during the global involvement in its fight for COVID-19. It has provided an opportunity for an already existing prejudiced attitude and behavior towards some communities and ethnic groups. Thus, in our current context, it calls for us humans to look for ways and measures to combat poverty, fear, anxiety, discriminatory acts, and behaviors, and xenophobia. In such a situation, how do we define relationships? Does Paul's call on redefining relationships have anything to say to us today in our uncertain, sad, broken, and fragile situation that we live in?

i. Redefining Relationships

The novel Coronavirus is redefining our relationship with one another and our physical space, i.e., geography by emphasizing distance, proximity, and hot spots. It has impacted areas and geographies interrupting our accessibility of things and affecting what humans have regarded as normal until now. Today the new normal that emphasizes social distancing has minimized our physical world by allowing us to confine only within the local space. Our physical connection is limited, but thanks to the technology that virtually we continue to connect with the rest of the globe. In an era of technology, we have the platform and space to work from home and continue to connect and contribute to our workforce. However, sadly the luxury of working from home is a far cry for many around the globe because of diverse reasons. Amid the global pandemic, we are also witnessing intensified cases of social stigma, xenophobia, fear, anxiety, and poverty. The fear and anxiety over the global pandemic are understandable, but what is worrying and unacceptable is discrimination and stereotyping. The pandemic is already a catastrophe, and so we must not allow fear and anxiety to breed xenophobia, bigotry, stigmatization, and discrimination. The great concern is also the impact of the pandemic on the global economy that could push millions into poverty.

Instead of discriminating, stigmatizing, and propagating hate speech and atrocities towards the other, it calls for us as humans to be in solidarity with one another and support one another. As evident in Paul's exhortation the ethic of love, hospitality and acceptance become important for us in our present situation of the global pandemic crises. Paul calls for love that is selfless and expects nothing in return. Today, amid the pandemic, we should live out and practice a love that transforms and accepts one another, a selfless love that creates and provides space for the "other," and guarantees a loving, peaceful environment. Such love provides a hospitable environment for reaching out in helping those undergoing difficult situations, in helping the needy, in taking time to listen, appreciate, and connect. Paul's exhortation on acceptance in the context of the Jewish and Gentile believers in Christ becomes relevant to our present situation and fight against the deadly global pandemic, the novel Coronavirus. Such a situation should provide us an opportunity to be supportive of one another, accept one another and aim towards collaborative networking in our fight against the virus, instead of stigmatizing, discriminating, and racial atrocities. As the world battles the global pandemic, an open and accepting community, ethnic/racial group, institutions, and religious bodies can be a model of transformation and hope. We can draw insights from Paul's exhortation of acceptance, for at the heart of it is the *notion of relationality*.

Bibliography

I. Ancient Texts and Translations

Biblia Hebraica Stuttgartensia. Stuttgart: Deutsche Bibelgesellschaft, 1977.

Cicero, M. Tullius. *De Officiis*, Edited by Walter Miller. http://www.perseus.tufts.edu (accessed on February 11, 2020).

Dio Cassius. *Roman History*. Translated by Ernest Cary. 9 vols. Loeb Classical Library. Cambridge, Mass: Harvard University Press, 1914-1927.

Josephus. Translated by H. St. J. Thackery et al., 10 vols. Loeb Classical Library. Cambridge: Harvard University Press, 1926-65.

Novum Testamentum Graece, NA 27. Stuttgart: Deutsche Bibelgesellschaft, 1996.

Orosius, Paulos. *History Against the Pagans*. http://www.attalus.org (accessed on March 11, 2020).

Philo. Translated by F. H. Colson et al. 10 vols. & 2 supps. Loeb Classical Library. Cambridge: Harvard University Press, 1929-62.

Seneca, *De Beneficious*. www.Perseus.tufts.edu (accessed on February 11, 2020).

Septuaginta, Rahlfs-Hanhart. NA: Hendrickson publishers, 2007.

Suetonius. Translated by J. C. Rolfe. 2 vols. Loeb Classical Library. Cambridge: Harvard University Press, 1997-98.

Tacitus, Cornelius. *The Annals*. http://www.perseus.tufts.edu (accessed on April 10, 2020).

II. Secondary Sources

Agosto, Efrain. “Patronage and Commendation, Imperial and Anti-imperial.” *Paul and the Roman Imperial Order*. Edited by Richard A. Horsely. London: Trinity Press International, 2004.

Barclay, John M. G. *Jews in the Mediterranean Diaspora: From Alexander to Trajan (323 BCE-117 CE)*. Edinburgh: T&T Clark, 1996.

Barclay, John M. G. *Paul and the Gift*. Grand Rapids, MI: William B. Eerdmans, 2015.

Barclay, John, M. G. “‘Neither Jew nor Greek:’ Multiculturalism and the New Perspective on Paul,” *Ethnicity and Bible*. Edited by Mark G. Brett. Biblical Interpretation Series. Vol. 19. Leiden/New York/Köln: E. J. Brill, 1996, pp. 198-214.

Barrett, C. K. *The Epistle to the Romans*. London: Adam and Charles Black, 1957.

Barton, Carlin. *Roman Honor: The Fire in the Bones*. Berkeley: University of California Press, 2001.

Bauer, Walter. *A Greek-English Lexicon of the New Testament and Other Early Christian Literature*. Translated by William F. Arndt & F. Wilbur Gingrich. 1958; Chicago/London: The University of Chicago Press, 1979.

Baur, Ferdinand Christian. *The Apostle of Jesus Christ. His life and Work, His Epistles and his Doctrine*. I. Translated by Eduard Zeller. 1876, Eugene, Oregon: Wipf and Stock Publishers, 2003.

Bendangjungshi. *Confessing Christ in the Naga Context: Towards a Liberating Ecclesiology.* Münster: LIT Verlag, 2011.

Black, D. A. "The Pauline Love Command Structure, Style and Ethics in Romans 12:9-21." *Filologia Neotestamentaria*, 2 (1989).

Bornkamm, Gunther. "The Letter to the Romans as Paul's last will and Testament." *The Romans Debate*, Edited by Karl Paul Donfried. Peabody, Massachusetts: Hendrickson Publishers, 1977.

Boyarin, Daniel. *A Radical Jew: Paul and the Politics of Identity*. Berkeley: University of California Press, 1994.

Broadhead, Edwin K. *Jewish ways of Following Jesus: Redrawing the Religious Map of Antiquity*. WUNT 266. Tübingen: Mohr Siebeck, 2010.

Brown, Raymond E. & John P. Meier. *Antioch and Rome: New Testament Cradles of Catholic Christianity*. New York: Paulist, 1983.

Burton, Ernest De Witt. *Syntax of the Moods and Tenses in New Testament Greek.* Chicago: University of Chicago, 1909.

Byrne, Brendan. *Romans*. SacPag, Vol. 6. Collegeville: The Liturgical Press, 1996.

Carter, Warren. *The Roman Empire and the New Testament: An Essential Guide.* Nashville: Abingdon, 2006.

Campbell, William S. *Unity and Diversity in Christ: Interpreting Paul in Context. Collected Essays*. Eugene, Oregon: CASCADE Books, 2013.

Carson, Donald A. *The Inclusive Language Debate: A Plea for Realism*. Grand Rapids: Baker, 1998.

Chow, John K. *Patronage and Power: A Study of Social Networks in Corinth*. JSNTSup. 75. Sheffield: JSOT, 1992.

Christensen, Duane L. *Deuteronomy 21:10-34:12.* WBC Vol. 6B. Nashville: Thomas Nelson Publishers, 2002.

Cranfield, C. E. B. *A Critical and Exegetical Commentary on the Epistle to the Romans*. ICC, 2 vols. Edinburgh: T&T Clark, 1975, 1979.

Cranfield, C. E. B. *Romans*. ICC, II. Edinburgh: T&T Clark, 1979.

Crook, Zeba. "Honor, Shame and Social Status Revisited," *JBL,* 128/3 (2009).

Das, A. Andrew *Solving the Romans Debate*. Minneapolis: Fortress Press, 2007.

Das, A. Andrew. "'Praise the Lord, All you Gentiles:' The Encoded Audience of Romans 15.7-13." *JSNT*, 34/1 (Sept 2011), pp. 90-110.

Deissmann, Adolf. *Light from the Ancient East: The New Testament Illustrated by Recently Discovered Texts of the Graeco-Roman World.* Translated by L. R. M. Strachan, 2nd edn. London: Hodder & Stoughton, 1927.

Delling, Gerhard. "λαμβάνω, ἀναλαμβάνω, ἀνάλημψις, ἐπιλαμβάνω, ἀνεπίλημπτος, κατα, μεταλαμβάνω, μετάλημψις, παρα-, προ-, προσλαμβάνω, πρόσλημψις, ὑπολαμβάνω." *TDNT*. Edited by Gerhard Kittel. Translated by Geoffrey W. Bromiley. vol. IV, Grand Rapids: WM. B. Eerdmans, 1967, pp. 5-15.

Delling, Gerhard. "τέλειος." *TDNT* vol. 8 Grand Rapids, MI: Wm B. Eerdmans 1972.

Domeris, W. D. "Sociology and Social Historical Investigations." in *Text and Interpretation. New Approaches in the Criticism of the New Testament.* Edited by P. J. Hartin & J. H. Petzer. Leiden: E. J. Brill, 1991.

Drane, J. W. "Why Did Paul write Romans?" *Pauline Studies. Essays Presented to Prof. F. F. Bruce on his 70th Birthday*. Edited by D. A. Hagner. Exeter: Paternoster Press, 1980.

Dunn, James D. G. *Romans 1-8*.WBC, 38A. Dallas: Word Books, 1988.

Dunn, James D. G. *Romans 9-16*, vol. 38b. WBC; Dallas: Word, 1988.

Dunn, James D. G. *The Acts of the Apostles*. Peterborough: Epworth press, 1996.

Dunn, James D. G. *The Theology of Paul the Apostle*. Grand Rapids, MI: William B. Eerdmans, 1998.

Elliott, John H. "Patronage and Clientage." *The Social Sciences and New Testament Interpretation*. Edited by *Richard* Rohrbaugh. Peabody, MA: Hendrickson, 1996.

Elliott, John H. *A Home for the Homeless. A Sociological Exegesis of 1Peter Its Situation and Strategy*. London: SCM Press, 1981.

Elliott, John H. *What is Social-Scientific Criticism?* Minneapolis: Fortress Press, 1993.

Elliott, Neil. *Liberating Paul: The Justice of God and the Politics of the Apostle*. Sheffield: Sheffield Academic Press, 1995.

Elliott, Neil. *The Arrogance of the Nations: Reading Romans in the Shadow of Empire*. Minneapolis, MN: Fortress Press, 2008.

Esler, Philip Francis. *Community and Gospel in Luke-Acts*. Cambridge: Cambridge University Press, 1987.

Esler, Philip Francis. *Conflict and Identity in Romans: The Social Setting of Paul's Letter*. Minneapolis: Augsburg Fortress, 2003.

F, Simon R. *Price, Rituals and Poor: The Roman Imperial Cult in Asia Minor*. Cambridge: Cambridge University Press, 1984.

Fishwick, D. *The Imperial Cult in the Latin West. Studies in the Ruler Cult of the Western Provinces of the Roman Empire*, vol. 3. Leiden & Boston: Brill, 2002.

Fitzmyer, Joseph A. *Romans: A New Translation with Introduction and Commentary*. New York: Doubleday, 1992.

Foerster, Werner "εὐάρεστος, εὐάρεστεω." *TDNT*. vol. 1. Grand Rapids, MI: Wm B. Eerdmans, 1985.

Furnish, V. P. *The Love Command in the New Testament*. London: SCM, 1972.

Garnsey, Peter. & Richard, Saller. *The Roman Empire: Economy, Society and Culture*. California: University of California Press, 2015.

Garnsey, Peter. *Social Status and Legal Privilege in the Roman Empire*. Oxford: Clarendon Press, 1970.

Garroway, Joshua D. "The Circumcision of Christ: Romans 15:7-13," *JSNT* 34/4 (June 2012), pp. 303-322.

Georgi, Dieter. *Theocracy in Paul's Praxis and Theology.* Minneapolis: Fortress Press, 1991.

Grundmann, Walter. "ἀγαθὸς." *TDNT*, vol. 1. Grand Rapids, MI: Wm B. Eerdmans, 1964.

Gupta, Nijay K. "What 'Mercies of God'? Oiktrimos in Romans 12:1 against its Septuagintal Background." *Bulletin for Biblical Research*, 22/1 (2012).

Gyekye, Kwame. *African Cultural Values. An Introduction*. Accra, 1996.

Hafemann, Scott. "Eschatology and Ethics. The Future of Israel and the Nations in Romans 15:1-13." *Tyndale Bulletin*, 51/2 (2000). pp. 161-192.

Richard S Hess, "rea" in *New International Dictionary of Old Testament Theology and Exegesis.* Edited by Willem A. VanGemeren, vol. 3. Grand Rapids, Michigan: Zondervan Publishing House, 1997.

Horsley, Richard A. (ed), *Paul and the Roman Imperial Order.* Harrisburgh, PA: Trinity Press International, 2004.

Horsley, Richard A. *Paul and Empire: Religion and Power in Roman Imperial Society.* Harrisburgh, PA: Trinity Press International, 1997.

Irons, Charles Lee. *A Syntax Guide for Readers of the Greek New Testament.* Grand Rapids, MI: Kregel.

Jervell, Jacob. "The Letter to Jerusalem." *The Romans Debate.* Revised and expanded edition. Edited by Karl Paul Donfried. 1977. Reprint, Peabody: Hendrickson, 1991, pp. 53- 64.

Jervis, L. Ann. *The Purpose of Romans: A Comparative Letter Structure Investigation*. Sheffield: JSOT Press, 1991.

Jewett, Robert and Roy David Kotansky. *Romans: A Commentary*, ed. Eldon Jay Epp, Hermeneia - a Critical and Historical Commentary on the Bible. Minneapolis, MN: Fortress Press, 2006.

Jewett, Robert. *Dating Paul's life*. London: SCM Press, 1979.

Kahl, Werner "Transgressing Boundaries: The Need for Intercultural Biblical Hermeneutics." *New Perspectives on Intercultural Reading of the Bible*. Edited by Daniel S. Schipani, Martien Brinkman & Hans Snoek. Elkhart, Indiana: A-VU University Amsterdam & Institute of Mennonite Studies, 2015.

Kallas, James. "Romans XIII:1-7: An Interpolation," *New Testament Studies*, 11 (1964-65), 365-374.

Käsemann, Ernst *Commentary on Romans*. Translated by G. W. Bromiley. Grand Rapids: Eerdmans, 1980.

Käsemann, Ernst. "Principles in the Interpretation of Romans 13." *New Testament Questions of Today*. Translated by W. J. Montague. Philadelphia: Fortress Press, 1969.

Kaster, Robert A. "The Shame of the Romans," *Transactions of the American Philological Associations*, vol. 127 (1997), pp. 1-19.

Keck, Leander E. "Christology, Soteriology, and the Praise of God (Romans 15:7-13)." *The Conversation Continues: Studies in Paul and John. In Honor of J. Louis Martyn*. Edited by Robert T. Fortna & Beverly R. Gaventa. Nashville: Abingdon Press, 1990, pp. 85-97.

Keesmat, Sylvia C. "If your enemy is hungry: Love and subversive politics in Romans 12-13," *Character and Ethics and the New Testament: Moral Dimensions of Scripture*. Edited by Robert L. Brawley. Louisville: John Knox Press, 2007.

Kim, Johann D. *God, Israel, and the Gentiles. Rhetoric and Situation in Romans 9-11*. SBL Study Series 176. Atlanta: SBL, 2000.

Kretzer, Armin. "λαμβάνω." *EDNT*. Edited by Horst Balz & Gerhard Schneider. vol. 2. Grand Rapids: William B. Eerdmans, 1991, pp. 336-338.

Kuhli, H. "Ἰσραήλ." *EDNT*, Edited by Horst Balz & Gerhard Schneider. vol. 2. Grand Rapids: William B. Eerdmans, 1991, pp. 202-204.

Kümmel, Werner Georg. *Introduction to the New Testament*. Translated and edited by H. C. Kee. London: SCM Press, 1966.

Kümmel, Werner Georg. *The New Testament: The History of the Investigation of its Problems*. Translated S. McLean Gilmore & Howard C. Kee. Nashville: Abingdon Press, 1972. German original, 1970.

Ladd, G. E. *A Theology of the New Testament*. Grand Rapids, MI: William B. Eerdmans, 1974.

Lampe, Peter. *From Paul to Valentinus: Christians at Rome in the First Two Centuries*. Translated by Michael Steinhauser, Edited by Marshall D. Johnson. 1989. Reprint, Minneapolis: Fortress Press, 2003.

Lendon, Jon E. *Empire of Honour: The Art of Government in the Roman World*. Oxford: Oxford University Press, 1997.

Ligt, L. de. *Fairs and Markets in the Roman Empire: Economic and Social aspects of Periodic Trade in a Pre-industrial Society*. Amsterdam: J. C. Gieben, 1993.

Lo Lung-Kwong. *Paul's Purpose in Writing Romans: The Upbuilding of a Jewish and Gentile Christian Community in Rome*. Hongkong: Alliance Biblical Seminary, 1998.

Lopez, D. C. *Apostle to the Conquered: Reimagining Paul's Mission*. Minneapolis, MN: Fortress Press, 2008.

MacDonald, Margaret Y. *The Pauline Churches. A Socio-historical Study of Institutionalization in the Pauline and Deutero-Pauline Writings*. SNTS MonographSer. 60. Cambridge: Cambridge University Press, 1988.

Malina, Bruce J. *The New Testament World: Insights from Cultural Anthropology*. 1981, London: SCM Press, 1983.

Marshall, Peter. *Enmity in Corinth: Social Conversations in Paul's Relation with the Corinthians*. Tübingen: Mohr Siebeck, 1987.

Mauss, Marcel. *The Gift: The Form and Reason of Exchange in Archaic Societies*. London: Free Press, 1954.

Meyer, Paul W. "Romans." in *Harper Collins Biblical Commentary*. Edited by James L. Mays. San Francisco, CA: Harper San Francisco, 2000, pp. 1038-1073.

Moo, Douglas. *The Epistle to the Romans*. NICNT. Grand Rapids: William B. Eerdmans, 1996.

Morris, Leon. *The Epistle to the Romans*. Grand Rapids, MI: William B. Eerdmans, 1988.

Moxnes, Halvor. "Honor and Righteousness in Rome," *JSNT* 32 (1988).

Moxnes, Halvor. "The Quest for Honor and the Unity of the community in Romans 12 and in the Orations of Dio Chrysostom." *Paul in his Hellenistic Context*, Edited by Troels Engberg-Pedersen. Edinburgh: T&T Clark, 1994.

Munro, Winsome. *Authority in Paul and Peter*. SNTS MonographSer 45. Cambridge: Cambridge University Press, 1983.

Murry, J. *The Epistle to the Romans.* NICNT; Grand Rapids, MI: William B. Eedrmans, 1975.

Nanos, Mark D. *The Mystery of the Romans. The Jewish Context of Paul's Letter to the Romans*. Minneapolis: Fortress, 1996.

North, Helen. *Sophrosyne: Self-Knowledge and Self-Restraint in Greek Literature*. Cornell Studies in Classical Philology, vol. XXXV. New York: Cornell University Press, 1966.

Nygren, A. *Commentary on Romans*. Translated by C. C. Rasmusser. 1944; London: SCM, 1952.

Oakes, Peter. (ed.) *Rome in the Bible and the Early Church*. Carlisle, Cumbria: Paternoster Press, 2002.

Oakes, Peter. *Reading Romans in Pompeii*. Minneapolis: Fortress Press, 2009.

Odyuo, Iris. "The various aspects of Naga art." *IOSR Journal of Humanities and Social Science*, 9/4 (March-April 2013), pp. 13-22.

Peterman, G. W. *Paul's gift from Philippi: Conventions of Gift Exchange and Christian Giving*. SNTSMS 92. Cambridge: Cambridge University Press, 1997.

Poythress, Vern S. "Male Meaning in Generic Masculines in Koine Greek," *Westminster Theological Journal*, 66/2 (2004), pp. 325-336.

Reasoner, Mark. *Strong and Weak. Romans 14:1-15:13 in Context*. SNTS MonographSer. 103. Cambridge: University Press, 1999.

Riesner, Rainer. *Paul's Early Period. Chronology, Mission Strategy, Theology*. Translated by Doug Stott. Grand Rapids: William B. Eerdmans, 1998.

Roetzel, Calvin J. "Sacrifice in Romans 12-15." *Word & World,* 6/4 (1986).

Rutgers, Leonard Victor. "Roman Policy toward the Jews: Expulsions from the City of Rome during the First Century C.E." *Judaism and Christianity in First-Century Rome*. Edited by Karl P. Donfried & Peter Richardson. Grand Rapids: William B. Eerdmans, 1998, pp. 93-116.

Ryken, L. Wilhoit & Longmann III. Dictionary *of Biblical Imagery: An Encyclopedic Exploration of the Images, Symbols, Motifs, Metaphors, Figures of Speech and Literary Patterns of the Bible.* Illinois: InterVarsity Press, 1998.

Sampley, J. Paul. *Paul in the Greco: Roman World: A Handbook.* Harrisburg, PA: Trinity Press International, 2003.

Sanday, William and Arthur Headlam. *A Critical and Exegetical Commentary on the Epistle to the Romans*. ICC. New York: Charles Scribner's Sons 1901.

Segal, Alan F. *Paul the Convert*. New Haven: Yale University Press, 1990.

Shohe, Zakali. "Redefining Relationships: The Role of the Spirit in Romans and its Significance in the Multiethnic Context in India." in *The Spirit over the Earth: Pneumatology in the Majority World*. Edited by Gene L Green, Stephen T. Pardue, K. K. Yeo. Grand Rapids, MI: William B. Eerdmans, 2016, pp. 58-77.

Shohe, Zakali. *Acceptance Motif in Paul: Revisiting Romans 15:7-13*. Frankfurt: Peter Lang, 2017.

Slingerland, H. Dixon. *Claudian Policymaking and the Early Imperial Repression of Judaism at Rome*. USF Studies in the History of Judaism 160. Atlanta: Scholars Press, 1997.

Smallwood, E. Mary. *The Jews Under the Roman Rule. From Pompey to Diocletian. A Study in the Political Relations*. Boston/Leiden: BRILL, 2001.

Stanley, Christopher D. *Arguing with Scripture: The Rhetoric of Quotations in the Letters of Paul*. New York: T&T Clark, 2004.

Stowers, Stanley. *A rereading of Romans: Justice, Jews and Gentiles*. New Haven: Yale University Press, 1994.

Talbert, Charles. "Traditions and Redactions in Romans XII. 9-21." *New Testament Studies*, 16 (1969-1970).

Taubes, Jacob. *The Political Theology of Paul*, Translated by Dana Hollander. 1993; Stanford: Stanford University Press, 2004.

Theissen, Gerd. *The Social Setting of Pauline Christianity: Essays on Corinth*. Edited and Translated by John H. Schütz. Philadelphia: Fortress Press, 1982.

Thompson, Michael. *Clothed with Christ: The Example and Teaching of Jesus in Romans 12:1-15:3*. JSNTSup. 59. Sheffield: JSOT Press, 1991.

Tobin, Thomas H. *Paul's Rhetoric in its Contexts. The Argument of Romans*. Peabody, Massachusetts: Hendrickson Publishers, 2004.

Toney, Carl N. *Paul's Inclusive Ethic: Resolving Community Conflicts and Promoting Mission in Romans 14-15*. WUNT 2, Reihe- 2252. Tübingen: Mohr Siebeck, 2008.

Wagner, J. Ross. *Heralds of the Good News: Isaiah and Paul "in Concert" in the Letter to the Romans*. NovTSup 101. Leiden: Brill, 2002.

Wallace, Daniel B. *Greek Grammer Beyond the Basics*. Grand Rapids: Zondervan Publishing House, 1996.

Walters, James C. "Romans, Jews and Christians: The Impact of Romans on Jewish/Christian Relations in First-Century Rome." *Judaism and Christianity in First-Century Rome*, Edited by K. P. Donfried & P. Richardson. Grand Rapids, Michigan: William B. Eerdmans, 1998.

Walters, James C. *Ethnic Issues in Paul's Letter to the Romans. Changing Self-Definitions in the Earliest Roman Christianity*. Pennsylvania: Trinity Press International, 1993.

Watson, Francis. *Paul, Judaism, and the Gentiles. Beyond the New Perspective*. Revised and expanded edition, Grand Rapids, MI: William B. Eerdmans, 2007.

Wedderburn, A. J. M. *The Reasons for Romans*. Edinburgh: T&T Clark, 1991.

Wengst, Klaus *Pax Romana and the Peace of Jesus Christ*. Translated by John Bowden. SCM Press, 1987.

Wiefel, Wolfgang. "The Jewish Community in Ancient Rome and the Origins of Roman Christianity." *The Romans Debate*, Edited by Karl Paul Donfried. Peabody, Massachusetts: Hendrickson Publishers, 1977.

Williams, Sam K. "Righteousness of God" in Romans," *JBL* 99/2 (1980), pp. 241-290.

Wink, W. *Engaging the Powers: Discernment and Resistance in a World of Domination*. Minneapolis, MN: Fortress Press, 1992.

Wong, Eric K. C. "The De-radicalization of Jesus' Ethical Sayings in Romans" in *Novum Testamentum*, 43/3 (2001), pp. 245-263

Zahn, T. *Introduction to the New Testament*. Edinburgh: T&T Clark, 1909.

Zahn, Theodore. *Der Brief des Paulus an die Römer*. Kommentar zum Neuen Testament 6. Leipzig: Deichert, 1910.

Zerbe, Gordon. *Non-Retaliation in Early Jewish and New Testament Texts: Ethical Themes in Social Contexts*. Bloomsbury: T&T Clark, 1993.

Ziesler, J. A. *Paul's Letter to the Romans*. TPI New Testament Commentaries; London: SCM, 1989.

III. Webliography

Jamir, M. Sashi. "The Impact of Modernization on the Nagas: Anthropological Analysis and Theological Response," 9-10, A thesis submitted to Asbury Theological Seminary, 2011. https://sashi2jamir.files.wordpress.com/2012/07/the-impact-of-modernization-on-the-nagas1.pdf (accessed on March 15, 2020).

Luithui, Shimreichon. "Naga: A People struggling for self-determination." https//:www.iwgia.org/images/publications// naga.pdf (accessed on March 15, 2020)

Marlowe, Michael D. "The Ambiguity of Anthropos," (2003). http://www.bible-researcher.com/anthropos.html (accessed on May 14, 2020).

Mosier-Dubinsky, Joy. "Women in Ancient Rome," *JCCC Honors Journal*, 4/2 (2013). https://scholarspace.jccc.edu/ cgi/viewcontent.cgi?article=1040&context=honors_journal (accessed on May 6, 2020).

Pohl, Christine D. "Hospitality, trust and reweaving the fabric of community." https://faith and leadership.com (accessed on December 9, 2019).

Spencer Elliott, "Political Paul and the Social Context of Romans 12-13," pp. 4-5. https://www.academia.edu (accessed on August 13, 2019).

Yinger, K. "Romans 12:14-21 and Nonretaliation in Second Temple Judaism: Addressing Persecution within the Community." (January 1998). *Faculty Publications-George Fox Evangelical Seminary*. Paper 62. https://digitalcommons.georgefox.edu/gfes/62 (accessed on March 27, 2020).

"Prevenient Grace:" The Theological Term for Hospitality. *Dotheword.org*.